THE **LITTLE BLACK BOOK** OF
LEADERSHIP

The Fundamental Skills Required
for Improving Yourself
and Successfully Leading Others

Todd Dewett, Ph.D.

TVA Inc.

Published by TVA Inc., PO Box 374, Dayton, OH 45409

Edited by Elizabeth Christensen
Proofread by Tina Yost
Graphic design by Carole Ohl

**Bulk discounts of this book are available upon request.
For more information contact Dr. Dewett at todd@drdewett.com.**

DR. DEWETT
FUEL FOR LEADERS®

My job is simple. I help people become leaders and I help leaders become better leaders. I am grateful that each year I have the opportunity to speak to, consult with, and train thousands. This book is a huge part of those efforts. It is a potent field manual that boils down a wealth of leadership wisdom into practical and useful chunks. It is the result of my business experience, training as a social scientist, and a good bit of caffeine. Enjoy. Find out more at **www.drdewett.com.**

Introduction

**Becoming a successful professional
requires a lot of hard work!**

Each day moves quickly and you need fast access to useful ideas to help you make the right decisions. That is what this book is all about: Simple, science-backed, proven tips and ideas to help you maximize your career potential and successfully lead others.

The scope of this book is uncommon. It covers the big picture of leadership and career success. For any paragraph or bullet in this book there are hundreds of books that dive into highly detailed treatments. Each of these books represents one or two pieces of the leadership puzzle. The book you are now reading helps you put all the pieces together to see a complete picture.

**Do not read this book and move on.
Use it as a reference, a conversation starter, and
a training aid.**

I wrote this book for hard-working professionals in the trenches who often need a dose of energy and a fresh perspective. It focuses on dealing with the context that surrounds you every day – your peers, your boss, and the people whom you lead.

**In the end, this book is a collection
of very simple ideas that will make,
or break you as a leader.**

Based on what I have seen, we could all use a refresher course – welcome to class.

THE LEADERSHIP OATH

Your journey begins after taking the following oath. Raise your right hand, repeat it aloud, and start living it immediately.

I believe leadership is a noble endeavor. Thus, I resolve to:

1. Improve myself and my organization, to better the professional lives of those whom I lead, and to productively impact the larger community.

2. Respect my employees and colleagues as important individuals, and to be open to their input and feedback when making decisions.

3. Realize the power of my example. Be very intentional and model a positive example every day.

4. Share credit widely, admit when I am to blame, and learn and grow from my mistakes.

5. Take calculated risks to advance myself and my organization. If I do not, I risk not reaching my potential.

6. Pursue learning as a fun, life-long task, and encourage continuous learning for others and for my organization.

7. Value personal responsibility and individual integrity as essential to my sustained success.

8. Be held accountable and hold others accountable based on our values, goals, and all applicable standards.

9. Be proactive when change is needed – be a part of the solution, not the problem. Recognize that great leaders and great organizations never rest on their laurels.

10. Make the best decisions possible for my organization, knowing that I cannot please everyone all the time, but that I can always seek to maximize the value I add to the organization.

HOW TO USE THIS BOOK

Honestly, at some point you need to read the entire thing! Recall that the point of this book is to string together a wide view of the many interesting facets of leadership.

However, it is also useful when you need a quick perspective on a specific topic and you only have five minutes. Flip to the appropriate page, digest a few bullets, and you are on your way.

Please note the "challenge" sections scattered throughout. Each is a pointed and very simple question or activity designed to make you consider how the ideas discussed here apply to your actual work. Growing as a leader is an active sport, so please take the challenges seriously and start playing with these ideas at work immediately.

THE **LITTLE BLACK BOOK** OF
LEADERSHIP

Table of Contents

1

LET'S KEEP THIS SIMPLE

THREE TYPES OF HUMANS

There are only three types of humans: people, experts, and geniuses. People do what experts tell them to do. Experts help people cope with reality. Geniuses create new realities. This book is not for geniuses. It is for experts and those striving to become experts who wish to improve their careers and their organizations.

Your goal is to be an expert leader.

Good news: you do not have to be a genius in order to be successful.

Success = 1/3 IQ, 1/3 effort, and 1/3 leadership skills.

IQ

Raw cognitive ability is terribly useful! However, it does have limitations. After a modest level of IQ, it ceases to be the most interesting differentiator among highly successful professionals. IQ matters, but only to a certain point.

Effort

This is a drastically underrated ingredient for professional success. Expending above average effort helps you learn more, helps establish a great long-term work ethic, and sends useful signals to others about how seriously you take your role as a professional.

There is always someone smarter than you,
but you can out work them any time you please.

Leadership Skills

This is the focus of the book you are reading: it addresses aspects of your professional development, the ability to communicate effectively, successfully motivate others, make high quality decisions, positively manage conflict, and effectively form and lead teams.

YOU HAVE BEEN DUPED

There are many not-so-useful leadership myths floating around that you should dismiss immediately. The biggest include:

- **Leadership is complex.** Not true. Nearly all leadership ideas and methods are simple. However, people can become complex to facilitate. Nonetheless, the list of things to do and tools to use are not, in and of themselves, complex.

- **Leadership is about "great men."** For many years there has been a love affair with iconic leaders who move mountains with their personality and will – "heroes." Bunk. Charismatic leaders are fascinating, but most successful leaders are not charismatic. The quiet, smart, and predictable leader can be just as successful. The trick is to understand your personal strengths, instead of trying to be something you are not.

- **Leadership is defined by big moments.** The big moments receive more attention – the key decision made in a crisis, the brave move to change strategic directions, the beauty of one great speech. Unfortunately, when we focus on these big moments too much we lose sight of what is most important – high-quality daily leadership. How your team reacts to you is determined by the daily average more than the big moments.
- **Leaders are born, not made!** Complete hogwash. It is true that intelligence and personality play an important role, but they only provide the foundation. How high you stand on top of that foundation is determined by how hard you work and the skills you develop.

A Practical Definition of Leadership

It is not complex or about being born a leader. Consider the following practical definition:

Leadership is the ability to achieve great personal and organizational results through others using positive interpersonal relationships.

Leadership is a series of skills. Success is the cumulative effect of many small daily decisions made using these skills. This set of skills is within the reach of anyone willing to invest the needed time.

MANAGER OR LEADER?

I propose we hereby kill the word "manager." Burn it, rip it up, stab it, it is done. It is heavily stigmatized as a "second-class citizen" compared to the idealized "leader."

Frankly, we simply do not need it. "Leader" will do. It is a big lie that "managers" and "leaders" are different things! Managers deal with the present. Leaders deal with the future. I am sure you have heard things like this before.

I actually found the list below on a website dedicated to helping United States government officials[1]:

- A manager takes care of where you are; a leader takes you to a new place.

- A manager deals with complexity; a leader deals with uncertainty.

- A manager is concerned with finding the facts; a leader makes decisions.

- A manager is concerned with doing things right; a leader is concerned with doing the right things.

- A manager's critical concern is efficiency; a leader focuses on effectiveness.

- A manager creates policies; a leader establishes principles.

---

[1] James Colvard. "Managers vs. Leaders,"
http://www.govexec.com/dailyfed/0703/070703ff.htm (July 7, 2003)

- A manager sees and hears what is going on; a leader hears when there is no sound and sees when there is no light.

- A manager finds answers and solutions; a leader formulates the questions and identifies the problems.

- A manager looks for similarities between current and previous problems; a leader looks for differences.

Hopefully, you see the humor and absurdity in these statements. In reality, managers and leaders are the same thing. However, there are many bad leaders!

Stop thinking about "manager" versus "leader," and start thinking about what it means to be a "great leader."

WHY YOU SHOULD CARE ABOUT THIS BOOK

If it is not already apparent to you that leadership skills are vital to your career, please consider these facts:

- **People voluntarily leave companies due to bad boss relationships.** Other factors matter, including: pay, need for opportunity, fit, etc. However, the biggest explanation by far is bad boss relationships. Nothing chases talent away faster.

- **How you are hired.** Yes, your track record matters, and yes, your education matters. Nonetheless, in the war for talent, the biggest deciding factor is people skills (many are addressed in this book). It is simple – when many people have good hard-side skills, the winner will have the best soft-side skills. It is up to you to build them and sell them.

- **How you are promoted.** It does matter that you are a great accountant if you want to become an accounting manager; however, the real test for most promotions is whether or not you have great people skills. Some are promoted based on hard-side skills only to fail because they lacked competence on the soft-side.

- **This is not just about you.** Organizations who understand the importance of these issues retain talent better and perform better. This is not just about your career. It is about making more amazingly productive companies.

WORTH THE BLOOD, SWEAT, & TEARS

If you work extremely hard to realize your potential as a professional and as a leader, you will undoubtedly experience numerous headaches and frustrations along the way. That is the beautiful nature of pushing yourself. However, the hard work and sacrifice are worth it. The monumental benefits include:

- The satisfaction of knowing you have pushed yourself to your limit.
- Gratitude from others whom you have developed and motivated.
- Kind words of support and encouragement from friends and colleagues who want you to succeed.
- Maximized earnings and opportunities for you and your loved ones to enjoy.
- Knowledge that your efforts helped maintain or create opportunities and security for other people.
- Pride in knowing you helped start and/or improved organizations with which you have been associated.

Those are among the best rewards in life.

Now let's get to work.

2

LEADERSHIP STARTS WITH YOU, NOT THEM

A QUICK GUIDE
TO SELF IMPROVEMENT

A short description of self improvement: understand yourself, set meaningful goals, and manage your time effectively. Before we dive into the details for each of these, we must address an old foe.

THE BLAME GAME

The BLAME game is an ongoing folly for many people and organizations. Real progress cannot begin until the BLAME ends.

BLAME is an acronym that stands for, "Barely Legitimate Almost Meaningless Excuse."

It is a partially true, yet wholly unproductive, process of faulting others instead of taking personal responsibility. Sadly, when you ask many professionals what the problem is, their index finger involuntarily thrusts outward to identify the culprit.

You must accept that a lot of the time, even if there is plenty of blame to go around, some of it is yours. Personal improvement will never happen if you do not stop the BLAME game.

PERSONAL RESPONSIBILITY, SELF-RELIANCE & SELF DISCIPLINE

The first step towards professional self-improvement involves a deep belief in personal responsibility, self-reliance, and self-discipline. These concepts will significantly influence the outcomes associated with everything you are a part of: tasks, projects, relationships, departments, business units, organizations – your entire career! They explain life success as much as career success.

Personal Responsibility

Who is responsible for how much you earn? Who is responsible for the evaluations you receive at work? Who is responsible for the skills you develop? The answers are not the economy, your boss, or the Human Resources department. The answer is you! To believe otherwise is dishonest, unproductive, and leads to playing the BLAME game.

Self-Reliance

It is true that teams can be amazingly wonderful. Nonetheless, you should not rely on team members more than you rely on yourself. You must use your own skills, capabilities, judgment, independence, and energy as the first and best assets in your career. Build yourself. Trust yourself. Believe in yourself.

Here is the best part: when you embrace self-reliance, you will find yourself building more positive and productive relationships and teams.

Self-Discipline

Self-discipline combines a long-term perspective with a strong will. It is the will to establish new patterns of personal behavior. It is the will to resist instant gratification while chasing difficult goals over protracted periods of time. It is the ability to force one's self to stay focused and on-track.

Sometimes people fail to reach goals not because the goals were too difficult, too vague, or because they lacked resources, but because they lacked the self-discipline to persist in the face of challenge.

UNDERSTAND YOURSELF

Understanding yourself requires you to engage in self-analysis in order to become more self-aware.

**Self-awareness is the cornerstone
of your professional development.**

The process begins with an understanding of five important issues about you: cognitive biases, personal values, personality, emotional intelligence, and professional strengths.

The better you understand these basics, the more you will be able to unlock the power of goal setting and rapid personal development.

Common Cognitive Biases

Here are my three favorite mental shortcuts that you need to avoid. Each is efficient, but rarely effective.

- **Self-biased assumptions.** This is the tendency to assume others think about a topic similarly to how you think about the topic. For example, a well-meaning boss might invite the team out for a cocktail – assuming they all like to drink alcohol. Maybe they do. Maybe they do not. Do not assume your co-workers share your views on politics, money, religion, or any significant work-related topic.

- **Positive Bias.** People usually overestimate themselves on a host of criteria. This affects decisions by injecting too much optimism. Consider that almost no one rates themselves poorly at work.

- **Stereotyping.** You often see people who "appear" to be a part of a particular group and you assume things about them based on that group affiliation. Thus, some might stereotypically think, "jock" = "dumb." An efficient thought, though rarely an effective conclusion. How often are you doing this without even realizing it?

These, and other, cognitive biases help you survive each day. We do not have time to think deeply about the many thousands of stimuli we encounter every day, and these shortcuts help us cope with that reality. These three, however, can get you in real trouble.

You never rid yourself of these mental shortcuts completely, but you can keep them in check if you are conscious of what they are and the fact that you are not immune to them.

CHALLENGE:

The next time you step foot in the office, look at the people around you and your list of current work projects. Take some mental notes. Where are you allowing these three filters to unproductively impact your work relationships?

Check Your Values

Next, you must get a clear grip on your personal and professional values. Most people say they know their values, but have real difficulty articulating them. What about you? Money? Family? God? People value many things.

CHALLENGE:

**Write down your top five values
in order of priority.**

If it takes you more than one minute, you need to get serious about articulating your values.

During your career, there is a 100% chance you will encounter the fabled "gray area" – that place where knowing right from wrong is not as clear as you wish it were. In the "gray area," any choice you make could have ugly implications. If you lack clarity about your values, you will make lower quality decisions.

Put the book down. Nail your list. A few minutes now will save you days or weeks later.

It is crucial to note that while pockets of professional activity exist where very questionable values are on display, it should go without saying that: 1) these are only small pockets, and 2) high personal integrity and strong values will increase your long-term odds of success significantly.

Personality

If you have not done so yet, take a popular personality test. There are many reasonably validated and readily accessible tools to choose from: DISC, MBTI, an assessment based on the Five Factor Model, etc. Speak with Human Resources to see what they have. Pick one.

Next, have your whole team take the test. Seriously consider hiring a well-trained professional to ensure that everyone understands what the tests say and what they do not say.

Please note: you are not trying to become a personality psychologist.

In terms of personal development, your simple goal is to develop a new vocabulary for understanding and talking about characteristic differences between you and others, and to gain insight into how others think about you. This type of knowledge very often stops or solves interpersonal conflicts and will increase your capacity to make effective decisions.

Emotional Intelligence

Emotional Intelligence (often referred to as EQ) refers to your ability to successfully assess and manage your emotions and others' emotions. This set of skills is considered equal in importance to IQ by most experts. In a leadership role, where interpersonal issues are so vital, EQ is a highly valuable skill commodity!

Emotions have a very strong influence over the outcomes of every situation. Both positive and negative emotions spread rapidly through groups at work, just like a virus.

**The people with the strongest ability
to make an emotional impact
are those in positions of leadership!**

Strong EQ allows you to take advantage of this reality in order to boost morale and productivity. Someone with high EQ perceives emotions accurately in others, feels empathy, tends to be more open and agreeable, and is less likely to engage in problem behaviors.

In contrast, if you or someone else lacks sensitivity to the emotional aspects of situations, has difficulty articulating thoughts related to emotions, or is unintentionally bully-like, there is a clear need to build additional EQ ability. Like personality, there are many useful and readily available tools.

Professional Strengths

You currently have a certain number of skills. Some skills are real strengths. Others are better described as not-so-strong. Your objective is to: 1) identify and build upon the strong skills, and 2) reduce any challenges associated with the not-so-strong skills.

First, what are your main strengths? They might include great writing ability, speaking skills, diffusing conflict, mathematical ability, knowledge of finance, creative problem-solving skills, facilitation skills, etc. There are endless possibilities. You can identify your main skill strengths several ways:

- **Self-Observation.** Time spent thinking deeply about one's professional performance. Think about your big wins and losses and those of the teams of which you have been a member. Most of your best strengths (and vice versa) should be evident.

- **Professional Outcomes.** Hard indicators provided by others that reflect on your professional abilities: jobs/roles assigned, promotions, raises, awards, and formal workplace evaluations. Together, when considered relative to your peers, they should begin to paint a picture of where you stand.

- **Feedback.** Informal performance-related information provided by your direct supervisor, peers, direct reports, mentors, clients, significant others, etc. Seek modest amounts proactively from others whom you trust to be bluntly honest and whom you feel have good insight into your performance and personality.

- **Assessments.** Instruments and activities designed to provide insight into your characteristic ways of behaving. Check your Human Resources department, or purchase them on your own. These include everything from popular books, surveys, facilitated and/or observed mock work activities (e.g., role play), computer driven activities and assessments, and observation of you on the job by relevant experts.

Second, what are your weak skill areas? Maybe you hate public speaking or will never for the life of you understand accounting.

We all have weak skill areas!

To focus on a weak skill area, consider three main strategies. First, you can dedicate time to improving these abilities. If you have trouble with public speaking, for example, join Toastmasters. Second, you can work over the long-term towards roles that rely less on your weaker skills. Finally, you should attempt to build teams of people who possess skills you do not possess.

CHALLENGE:
Identify your top three skill strengths and at least one main skill weakness.

PERSONAL GOAL SETTING

Once you have completed your skill assessment, it is time to engage the most powerful process in the world of professional development: goal setting.

Later, we will address setting goals for others. Right now, I want you to think about setting goals for yourself. I am not referring to formal goals created with, or by your boss at work. I am referring to goals you set for yourself which may, or may not, overlap with your formal work goals.

Goals are the single most important tool for improving individual and group performance.

Goals direct attention and focus limited resources towards desired ends. As a result, they increase the odds of reaching the outcomes you target.

First, we will define the three major types of goals, then address goal characteristics, and finally the goal-setting process.

As you think through your goals, keep in mind what you learned from your self-analysis – especially your biggest values, your personality, and professional strengths. They should influence the goals you set and how you pursue them.

Three Types of Goals

The three major types of goals are: performance goals, leadership goals, and life goals.

Performance goals are focused on the "hard side" of the organizational equation – the actual tasks and projects to be completed. They concern your work accomplishments over a specific time period. As you grow in your career, be sure to consider these different forms of performance goals:

- **Functional.** Goals related to one or more of the major business functions of the organization (accounting, marketing, operations, sales, etc.).

- **Task/Process.** Goals related to core processes and their components within one function (e.g., Accounts Payable within the Accounting function) or across multiple functions (e.g., New Product Development).

- **Level**. Goals concerning your vertical position in the hierarchy. Are you providing input to a team managing a process? Do you want to lead the team? Do you want to lead multiple teams, processes, or departments? Do you want to be an executive?

In general, as an example, look at the first third of your career as primarily focused on becoming a financial professional (functional goal) with strong capital budgeting and investor relations abilities (task/process goals) while mapping out a path towards becoming a Vice President of Finance (level goal).

Your approach to the remainder of your career depends entirely on your personal interests, need for achievement, and tolerance for stress: either gain new functional and task/process abilities or focus more heavily on level. There is no perfect path.

You must define a path forward that will maximize your chances of being happy.

Leadership Goals are focused on the "soft side" of the organizational equation – the areas of professional expertise and knowledge that either help or hurt your pursuit of performance goals.

The most important leadership skill areas include effective communication, goal setting, problem solving and decision making, motivating others, and the rest of the major topics in this book.

Goals in this area also include any and all educational objectives achieved via educational institutions, various forms of training, mentoring, or self-study.

Life Goals concern your long-term happiness. It is monumentally important to include life goals in addition to performance and leadership goals. They include major financial milestones, work/life balance, leisure needs, geographical preferences, family considerations, and any other important life matters you wish to address.

What good is spectacular career achievement without equally amazing life achievement?

Your life goals should be designed to ensure that you are as healthy and happy as possible after having pursued your performance and leadership goals. They are the "yin" to your career "yang." What they are is up to you, though one is absolutely mandatory: career "fit."

Career rule #1 is to pursue your passions and interests, and to maximize the use of your strengths.

This represents your best chance to be both happy and successful. Unfortunately, too many people pursue occupations and careers based on the desires and beliefs of others – do not be like them.

CHALLENGE:
Can you articulate your 2-, 5-, and 10-year goals?

Goal Characteristics

Remember that all goals must be SMART: specific, measurable, aligned, reachable, and time bound.

- **Specific.** Be very finite. Do not say "improve" when you can say "increase by 50% before the third quarter." Do not say "grow the business" when you can say "grow revenues by 20% in three years with 50% of growth from new products."

- **Measurable.** It is true what they say: you can't manage what you can't measure. You must think ahead when goal setting and be sure that measurement is possible without being unnecessarily difficult or burdensome. Metrics should be as simple as possible.

- **Aligned.** Be sure that achieving one goal does not undermine your ability to achieve other goals. Ideally, different personal goals are at least modestly related and thus, mutually supportive.

- **Reachable.** All goals should be at least modestly challenging. If they are too easy you will not strive as hard as you should – no new skills or knowledge gained. In contrast, goals that are too difficult can quickly become demotivational.

- **Time Bound**. Specify the "due date" or you are guaranteed to take more time than is needed! This applies to each goal and associated milestones. Depending on how progress unfolds, timelines can be adjusted.

A Personal Goal-Setting Process

There are five main steps in the personal goal-setting process: defining your goals, identifying milestones, tracking progress, communicating progress, and administering self-rewards. As the old saying goes, a chain is only as strong as its weakest link – do not neglect any of these steps.

- **Defining Your Goals.** Keep in mind, there is no perfect mix of goal types. Through trial and error you will find the combination that works best for you. This combination will change over the course of your career. Similarly, there is no "correct" number of goals. Starting with only a few is a safe place to begin.

- **Identifying Milestones.** Each of your goals must be broken down into the major tasks/projects/components to be achieved, in chronological order. These subparts show you the basic path to goal achievement.

- **Tracking Progress.** Document the milestones and goals over time using whatever mechanism you prefer: personal notes, a spreadsheet, project management software, etc. Depending on how your progress unfolds, reassess/redefine your goals periodically as required.

- **Communicating Progress.** Ideally, you need one or two key confidants with whom you can discuss your goals and your progress towards achieving your goals. You will be more successful if you "go public" with your personal goals.

- **Administering Self-Rewards.** Believe in delayed gratification. Think about the material objects you desire or simple daily indulgences such as ice cream or your favorite television program. Tie their acquisition or consumption to goal achievement (or at least major milestone achievement). You must "earn" these things through your performance relative to your goals.

CHALLENGE:
Name a person or two you will use when you "go public" with your goals.

As you craft your goals, recall that there are many ways to learn, opportunities to gain experience, and chances to build skills. Beyond normal learning while on the job, these include:

- **Educational Degrees.** You must have at least one college degree in today's world. If you do pursue a degree, remember two things: First, the network you build while in school is as important as the material you learn. Second, quality of education is more important than convenience.

- **Non-Degree Certifications and Credentials.** Depending on your career path, these might include PHR, PMP, CFP, CSCP, CPIM, or many others – look them up!

- **Mentors.** A good mentor has high character, above average interpersonal "soft-side" skills, above average functional job skills, and a solid track record of performance. If they are worth having as a mentor, they are busy and may not have much time. Find them, offer to help them if possible, and seek their advice.

- **Observation.** Never underestimate the power of vicarious learning. That refers to learning by watching as opposed to learning by doing. If you watch your boss or a colleague in a meeting or out in the cube farm, but you are not actually interacting with them, there is no risk for you in the situation. Thus, you learn unencumbered by the need to think about what you will say next, or how you will respond to a comment.

- **Training – they pay**. This is not about new initials after your name. It is about taking classes or seminars (live, virtual, or blended) to build new hard or soft skills. This is useful for your current job and for your resume. Check with your boss and/or Human Resources and find out what relevant training your organization offers internally or will pay for externally and sign up.

- **Training – you pay.** If your organization has a razor thin training budget, yet you have identified an important skill area to pursue, scrounge up your own pennies and pay for the training yourself. Think big picture here – shouldn't you invest more in yourself than anyone else?

- **Volunteer**. You can volunteer at work or for other organizations (e.g., your church, non-profits, community groups, organizational boards, professional associations). This can help you learn new functional skills, and it is a great way to build leadership skills and your professional network while also sending a positive signal about how much you value professional service.

- **Expanded opportunities at work.** Ask for new or additional responsibilities, maybe a "stretch" assignment. Use the opportunity to add value to the organization while acquiring new skills for yourself. Bonus benefit: next time you ask for a raise you are more likely to receive it.

- **Read! Read! Read!** Do not give me that "I'm too busy" stuff. They do not all have to be business books, but a nice share should be. There are thousands to choose from. Start by looking at business bestseller lists.

CHALLENGE:
If you are not reading at least 5-10 books per year, pick up the pace.

- **Start a group at work.** A book club, a social networking group, a brown bag lunch series, a group dedicated to sharing various "hard" skills, a group for discussing "soft" skills, etc. This is both about gaining new knowledge and expertise, and improving your network.

TIME MANAGEMENT

Step one for professional improvement is self-analysis, step two is goal setting, and now step three: determining how to use your time in a manner that maximizes your odds of goal achievement and career success.

Most professionals tell me they never have enough time to do everything they wish to do in a given day, week, or month.

That is bull. They simply have not used the available time correctly.

There are three main issues that you have to contend with if you want to control time instead of allowing time to control you: the 80/20 Rule, when to work on what, and how to guard your time.

The 80/20 Rule

This classic is all about prioritizing. To prioritize means to place something ahead of something else. Seems simple, but it paralyzes many professionals. Think of all of the people, tasks, and projects that dominate your typical week or month.

CHALLENGE:
Write down the top 20 things you have to do at work. Which things on your list are the least important? Mark them off the list. Try marking off at least half of the list using this rule.

It becomes brutal fast – which is why you have to spend time identifying the most important people, tasks, and projects (the 20%).

The 80/20 Rule, also known as the Pareto Principle, is invaluable as a place to begin thinking about many issues. Eighty percent of the work is done by 20 percent of the people, eighty percent of the profits come from 20% of the products, etc.

I am not telling you to neglect the less important people, tasks, and projects (the 80%). The point is to make sure you identify and focus on the things that matter most. The 20 percent represents a very special group of people, tasks, and projects that will determine how fast and how far you will climb the organizational ladder.

To identify the 20 percent, ask yourself these two important questions:

- Which tasks/projects will bring you the most experience, new relationships, and best visibility? Translated: what type of work or which functional areas usually provide the "fast track" in your organization? Ideally, they will align with your personal strengths so that you do not lose too much "fit."

- Which relationships should be newly established, more fully developed, or deemphasized? Translated: who you hang around matters a lot! Find the most productive networks of people at work and figure out how to join them.

Look at your list again. In fact, write down one week's worth of typical tasks and activities. Which are the most important for your future in the organization and in your career? These are the 20%. Give them a check mark. Now make an honest estimate of the amount of time you spend on the items you did not mark.

You might be amazed by how much time and effort you are putting into the 80%. Find the 20% and treat it with the reverence it deserves.

CHALLENGE:

Try not to spend more than half of your time on the 80%.

When to Work on What

Once you have the 20% clearly in sight, it is time for step two. When is the best time to work on these things? Think carefully and determine the two or three hour window each day when your brain processes most effectively. It is the time of day you are able to think through complex challenges without getting a headache. This is your Einstein Window.

CHALLENGE:

Identify when you have your daily mental peak and dedicate it to the 20%.

I realize you face constraints – you have meetings, calls to make, and employees who need you. An occasional distraction is inevitable, but the rule is to work vigorously to protect the Einstein Window. Most of the time you think superficially. Only during the Einstein Window do you have good odds of breakthrough thinking.

How to Guard Your Time

There are many simple ways to protect the amazing Einstein Window. Here are just a few:

- **If you have one, close the door**. Open-door management has its limits. Keep it open most of the day, but close it when you are working on the "good stuff" during those precious few hours when your brain really excels.

CHALLENGE:
Keep the door closed at least one hour each day.

- **Turn off all manner of devices** that will chirp or beep and distract you.

CHALLENGE:
Turn off the ringer on the phone at least one hour out of each day (during the Einstein Window) and only check email a few times each day.

- **You must learn to say, "No."** "No" is not a four-letter word. How many times have you been deep in thought when your boss or a peer wanders in and asks for help with something that is not an emergency? If it is during your "Einstein Window" and not an emergency, say "No" and get back to them later.

CHALLENGE:

Track how often you say no. You may be shocked how rarely you use the word.

- **Get lost if needed**. Literally. Get away from the people hogging your time and set yourself free! Take the occasional Einstein Window, and a meaningful chunk of your 20%, and leave your cube or office. Take your retreat in an empty conference room or at the park down the street – get creative.

CHALLENGE:

Identify at least three places – other than your office – where you can go to work during the Einstein Window.

You can manage your time more effectively by following the rules above. However, it is important to note a related issue.

You will work more hours than everyone else if you wish to be abnormally successful.

That means the old saying, "work smarter not harder" is not the best advice. You need to do both. If the hours scare you, leadership is not your game.

Personally, nothing inspires me more than stories of entrepreneurs working on new businesses in their basement at night while toiling away in cubeville by day. Or, how about the marathoner who trains before work, at lunch, and after work?

There is no shortage of examples of people doing what it takes to realize their dreams. Step away from the television and get to work!

3

DEWETT'S RULES

This chapter is about the three most important daily leadership rules to live by. They are the three general ideas that tie together everything else. Do not simply read them – commit them to memory:

REDUCE AMBIGUITY

BE FAIR

STAY POSITIVE

Great ideas, tools, tactics, practices and methodologies mean nothing unless you know how to get value out of them, which requires understanding successful ways to deal with people.

The best way to deal with people successfully is to: reduce ambiguity, be fair, and stay positive.

Never forget that the most important influence on employee morale and productivity is the quality of the relationships that surround the individual every day.

The most important relationship by far is the relationship between the employee and their direct supervisor.

Ask yourself if you have done enough, every day, to reduce ambiguity, be fair, and stay positive when you:

- Talk to peers or employees
- Participate in, or facilitate a meeting
- Make a telephone call
- Send an email
- Give a presentation
- Write a memo or report
- Leave a voice message
- Post to a blog
- Speak with a customer
- Text, IM, etc.

In short, whenever you are communicating, briefly consider all three! Now, on to the details for each rule...

RULE 1 – REDUCE AMBIGUITY

The first rule is all about effective communication. Your goal is to learn to communicate in a manner that reduces the ambiguity experienced by others.

Ambiguity refers to uncertainty about what has happened, what might happen next, or how to proceed. The punch line is simple:

At work, people hate not knowing and not understanding.

It is a simple concept with massive implications. At every turn, employees have the potential to experience ambiguity – when you give them the opportunity.

What happens when people sense ambiguity? Lots of things you do not want to happen. When people experience ambiguity at work, they experience negative emotions (e.g., fear, doubt, anger, anxiety, or suspicion). When they lack information or understanding and begin experiencing these fun emotions, they tend to make false assumptions about your meaning or intentions.

The employee is experiencing ambiguity, the negative emotions kick in, they make erroneous assumptions – then what? Their performance suffers. Becoming a better communicator reduces the likelihood that you will create these unproductive outcomes.

THE BASICS OF EFFECTIVE COMMUNICATION

One of the most important catalysts for improved performance is great performance-related conversations. To have a great conversation, you must understand the elements of effective communication. Good news: communicating effectively is legitimately viewed as a set of skills. Skills are learned.

Know your audience

This may be the most important rule since every communication context varies in terms of the expected speaking style, use of different aids or technologies, attire, etc. From email to phone call to formal speech, first consider your audience.

Though different communication contexts sometimes require different approaches, in general, if a communication episode involves speaking, keep the following in mind:

- **Use a moderate or strong volume.** Good volume is a must for anything beyond an intimate interpersonal conversation. For any group or presentation context, it is vital.

- **Avoid being monotone.** Consistently high volume, odd as it may seem, can be just as bad as consistently low volume. Some variance is required to maximize message impact. Variance should swing the highest around the most important points.

- **Articulate words clearly.** Your ability to enunciate or pronounce words clearly is explained by innate skill, educational training, and message practice and rehearsal. When in doubt, practice more, not less.

- **Nail the grammar**. Using double negatives, improper subject-verb agreement, or any other common form of improper grammar will create unwanted impressions about your intelligence and competence. This also includes the need to reduce or eliminate the use of "um" and "uh" as nervous fillers.

CHALLENGE:
Be brave and appoint someone to regularly point out your bad grammar.

- **Pace yourself modestly.** Too slow, they go to sleep or become impatient. Too fast, they can struggle to keep up. Someone other than yourself is typically better than you at judging the adequacy of your pace. Practice communicating in front of an honest friend or colleague and ask their opinion.

- **Avoid excessive slang or jargon.** The appropriateness of slang or jargon varies by context. Know the norms of communication for a given context and speak appropriately. Do not say, "stuff" or, "you know" when in front of executives and do not discuss "core competencies" with a Boy Scout troop.

Formal presentations follow additional rules, though for most communication needs involving your voice, these will suffice.

Next, let's consider the actual words you choose. Effective communication at work is honest, specific, concise, supportive, timely and contains a heavy dose of listening by all parties involved.

- **Be Honest**. Honesty is usually the most ethical and the most effective choice. When your outer voice is consistent with your inner voice, people sense the sincerity. Also, whether the message is positive and affirming or necessarily critical, people accept it better when you "own" it. No passing the buck to "the group," "the committee," "the policy," or "corporate." There are exceptions, but this is a great general policy.

- **Be Specific.** This means be precise, clear, and articulate – not general. How many times has someone told you, "good job" or "this will do" or "we'll talk later?" These comments are vague and difficult to interpret. Strive for concrete language that someone can easily understand and visualize. Do not say someone was unprofessional when you actually meant that his shirt was wrinkled, he was late, and he used excessive slang. If you want people to actually listen to you, try being very specific.

- **Be Concise.** This refers to brevity – saying just the right amount. Say too much, you will overload your audience. Going "off topic" confuses people. The goal is for your audience to understand you and remember your message. Only then does your message have a chance to add any value.

- **Be Supportive.** This means to be appreciative of someone's comments and to respond to their suggestion in an affirmative manner. However, being supportive is not the same as complimenting someone. You always support their participation – you sometimes support the actual content they offer. Always say things such as, "Thanks for the comment, I will have to consider that," or "I had not thought of that." Based on what you actually think, you might say, "Thanks! That is a great idea!"

- **Be Timely.** This refers to when and how often to communicate. When do you give feedback, provide advice, or tell employees about changes to processes or policies? As soon as possible. If feedback is not provided very close in time to the performance in question, it will not be useful. Human memory is very limited. Do not delay important conversations.

Your Body Speaks Louder Than Your Words

Effective communication is not only about the words you use, but the things you do while using them. Half of the meaning you convey in a communication episode does not come from your words. In general, there are three regions of the body to consider in most communication contexts:

- **Below the Waist.** (Important) From the waist down: your main goal is to remove this region of the body from the equation. Leave your feet planted, no rocking back and forth. Leave the hips stationary, no swaying – keep your weight balanced. It is the least important area of the body for conveying meaning. Do not allow it to become a distraction.

- **Waist to Shoulders**. (Very important) Square your shoulders to face the person (or swivel as needed to scan the audience). Stand up straight! Hands/arms: creating motions to complement your words is the best strategy. There are many common gestures to use and to avoid. Consider these:
  - **Poor choices**: arms crossed in front or hands clasped together in the back (both convey a closed rigid demeanor), hands in pockets (usually conveys excessive informality).

- **Acceptable choices**: arms sitting motionless at your side (not adding to your speech, but not detracting), hands clasped in front of you with at least a little use of hands and arms to convey meaning (be sure to avoid "washing" or wringing your hands nervously).
- **Great choices**: allow your hands/arms to complement your words; use a fist to emphasize a very important point, show small numbers (1-10) on your hands in addition to saying them aloud, turn your hands up and show your palms when asking the audience a question, etc.
- **Head.** (Most important) By far the most potent nonverbal cues come from the neck up. Two must be noted above all else: eye contact and smiling. Eye contact conveys confidence, competence, and focus. Lack of eye contact tends to convey a lack of confidence, nervousness, and a lack of preparation. Smiling projects positive emotion and engagement – these productively amplify your message. Emotions are contagious – it is difficult not to smile back when someone smiles at you!

CHALLENGE:

Have someone videotape you at work – running a meeting, giving a presentation, talking to a customer. You will learn a lot by reviewing yourself on video.

How to Listen Effectively

This topic is so important it deserves a little more than one bullet. It has been said that we have two ears and one mouth for a reason. Great communication is not always about you speaking.

What do most listeners in a one-on-one conversation actually do? Do we actively process what is being said and focus on the message? No. Most of us are not actually listening. This is even more likely when we are talking to our boss or someone with more expertise or authority.

We stop listening after the first few sentences and begin thinking deeply about what in the heck we are going to say in return to dazzle and impress. We sometimes do this so much, we actually miss the key points being communicated!

To improve your listening skills, try the following:

- **Get Focused.** Stop multi-tasking. Multi-tasking is drastically overrated. Stop reading email, stop reading that report, put down the pen or smart phone, look the person in the eyes, and listen to what they are saying.

- **Stop Judging.** Allow them to finish delivering the message without making value judgments concerning how you feel about their position on the issue. Too much judging and you will not accurately hear what they are trying to say. A little judging is inevitable, but keep it in check.

- **Stop Replying Early.** Prematurely responding inside your head is the main result of making early judgments. The more time you spend mentally crafting your response, the more time you will miss out on what they are saying, increasing the odds that your response is not appropriate. Pay attention!

- **Take Some Notes.** There are two huge benefits associated with taking notes. One, notes are a hedge against poor memory. Two, this behavior sends a signal about how seriously you are listening to their message. In the moment, identify and jot down two, three, or four important things they are saying by capturing them with as few words as possible.

- **Close by Summarizing.** When the focus again switches back to you, it is often useful to use your memory and your notes to summarize the message so you can ask them if you accurately heard their message. Again, two huge benefits: One, a chance to increase the accuracy of your understanding; two, you send another great signal.

Choosing Communication Channels Wisely

There are many channels of communication. Each offers a mix of efficiency and effectiveness. Efficiency refers to how fast the channel is capable of relaying a message. Effectiveness refers to the channel's ability to deliver meaning.

Your goal:
never sacrifice effectiveness for efficiency.

When in doubt about which channel to use, choose a higher-quality option. Consider these categories of common channels:

- **High effectiveness, variable efficiency** – Face-to-face or video conference. The best channel by far for message effectiveness is face-to-face. No other channel offers high quality, "real-time" ability to correct yourself, ask questions, repeat and summarize, read nonverbals, etc.

- **Modest effectiveness, modest efficiency**. Telephone or teleconference. Hearing a voice can be powerful. While visual cues are not present on a phone call, a significant amount of verbal cues are.

- **High efficiency, variable effectiveness**. Voice message, electronic mail, text messages. These offer great convenience and efficiency, but they are questionable. Believe me: emails and text messages are overrated in terms of their ability to convey precise meaning.

To summarize the ideas above: face-to-face trumps the telephone and the telephone trumps electronic mail.

No amount of odd fonts or animations in an email will ever come close to providing the range and complexity of meaning expressed by actual humans in person!

Think for a moment about how often you rely on channels with low capacity and you will begin to understand the lost opportunity to correctly convey messages as you intended.

CHALLENGE:

Share a small sample of emails and reports with a colleague (who was not the recipient) and have them show you where you unintentionally added ambiguity.

You are likely to be amused by how your words are interpreted!

Additional Communication Tips

The basics are clear enough, though it is useful to remember a few extra facts. Let's start with the 80/20 rule discussed earlier. It is not reasonable for you to do everything suggested in this book all the time. It is, however, reasonable to try to follow all of these guidelines when you are dealing with the 20%.

Here are a few other great communication pointers for any leader:

- **Praise in public, punish in private.** A classic leadership and communication maxim. I do not like the word "punish" but the point is a great one. Praise openly, yet reprimand while trying to help the person save face.

- **Sensitive message, sensitive delivery.** The more sensitive the message, the more you need to strive for private surroundings and face-to-face delivery (or the most effective channel available).

- **Important message, rehearsed message.** The more important the issue or episode, the more you should prepare and practice. Get more than one pair of eyes (and ears) involved in your practice efforts if this is a 20% issue.

- **When in doubt, choose a better channel.** If you ever find yourself editing an email longer than it took to write it – cancel the message and pick up the phone. If you ever feel like emailing instead of talking to someone – walk to their office and talk to them!

- **When angry, do not communicate.** Never speak to someone directly, call them, or email them when you are upset. This never helps. Similarly, if you are communicating and real anger sets in, walk away from the situation. Communicate only after you calm down.

- **Do not act like you know something you do not know.** People do not like "know-it-alls" and they usually sense that someone is making things up. Yet they love authenticity. Admit you do not know the answer, find the answer, and get back to them.

Transparency Reduces Ambiguity

Aside from effective communication, here is another gem to keep in mind about ambiguity – no hiding or hoarding information. People generally hate surprises.

Sharing information widely is a fundamental part of building positive relationships. Hoarding information due to autocratic tendencies, or for political reasons tends to do just the opposite.

When your budget gets cut, tell your people. When a policy changes that you know they will not like, tell them. Sooner than later. In fact, make sure they know that you are involved in a discussion about the issue before you even know what the outcome will be, and let them know what you are advocating for and why.

When things get tough at work (e.g., budget cuts, reorganizations, personnel reductions) many leaders fear conflict and tend to begin hoarding information even more than usual. At some level this is understandable, but it is not the right answer.

The more difficult situations become, the more transparency you need.

Otherwise, you will amplify the ambiguity others experience and will kill their productivity.

RULE 2 – BE FAIR

Everyone seems to have a different idea about what fairness means. Let's start by talking about what fairness is not.

Fairness is not simply the "Golden Rule."

Organizations are bureaucratic hierarchies. Everyone is not equal and should not be treated equally. Fairness does not mean paying everyone the same or even similar salaries. It does not mean recognizing everyone in very similar ways so that no one feels left out.

People do care deeply about the outcomes they receive (e.g., raises, promotions, new projects, praise, punishments), the process used to make these decisions, and how they are actually treated as people with respect to these decisions. People do not expect equal outcomes (i.e., they do not always have to win), but they do want to be informed and respected. That is fair!

You should care about this because when an employee senses a lack of fairness, ugly things can happen – even with regard to what you feel is a small issue. The three biggest outcomes you would like to avoid are:

- **They try to change the outcome.** For example, maybe they feel their raise was too low. Expect them to try to change the outcome by speaking directly to you (and to others about you).

- **They get lazy.** Continuing with the same example, if they do not want to take the risks associated with discussing their pay, maybe they simply start, "phoning it in." They come in late, leave early, or surf the internet more.

- **They make things up.** Here, they psychologically distort reality to fit their needs. They assume their low raise was due to budget problems and that everyone received smaller than expected raises. They dream up an explanation that allows them to feel sane and modestly satisfied.

All three of these represent hits to morale and productivity. You must avoid them.

The answer is that to be fair you must treat people the same and not the same at the same time.

Treat them the same by:

- Creating a **positive** and **productive** work environment for everyone.

- Making decision processes and resource allocations **transparent to all**.

These are the acceptable ways to treat everyone the same. In a fair work environment, people are positive and how someone obtains valued outcomes is understood, and outcomes are not determined based on favoritism or randomness.

Next, treat people differently by:

- Examining individual and group performance **honestly and regularly**.

- Recognizing and rewarding people based on **performance**.

You cannot tell everyone they are exceptional or a "Superstar." However, you can always explain yourself, show gratitude for good efforts, and say 'thank you.' Make the vast majority of your recognition and rewards contingent on strong performance.

Explanations, Participation, and Bull

To reduce perceptions of unfairness, offer quality explanations for the decisions you make. This is especially true if you follow the "contingent on performance" mantra instead of some misguided belief in equality.

A good explanation may not make someone love what has happened, but it goes a long way towards getting them to accept what has happened as legitimate.

Building on the characteristics of effective communication discussed earlier, a great explanation is:

- **Honest**. Reveals the actual thought process used. Never forget: most people easily sense insincerity.
- **Owned**. You take responsibility personally instead of, "passing the buck." Owning your message leads to increased respect.
- **Timely**. The rule is simple: the sooner the better. The more time elapses, the less an explanation will help – even if it is a great one.

You have two types of situations to deal with in terms of managing perceptions of fairness:

- **A bonafide leadership issue.** In this type of situation it is not normal or expected to seek employee input (e.g., many compensation-related issues). Strive for transparency to craft useful explanations.

- **A voice opportunity.** These are times when it is normal and expected to have employee input during the process (e.g., hiring situations, individual and group goal setting). Participation is required – but you still owe great explanations come decision time.

Often there may be a difference of opinion defining the type of situation you are dealing with! Leaders are more likely to think they are dealing with the first type, and employees, more often than not, are going to think it is the latter.

CHALLENGE:

When in doubt, and if there is adequate time, assume you will benefit from soliciting genuine employee input.

To be honest, all participation opportunities are not created equal. There are two types. I call them real participation and bull.

- **Real participation.** First, it is sought with the intention of actually hearing what the employees think, as opposed to simply managing impressions. Second, there is an honest intention to consider acting on the employee input.

- **Bull.** It lacks both of the attributes noted above. Here, leaders have failed to realize most employees can sense insincerity. Plus, if never listened to, employees stop offering input, start saying what they think the boss wants to hear, or they simply shut up altogether.

Share the Pain

Another great way to build a positive perception of fairness is to "share the pain." When people feel they are in an ugly and unfair situation with others, instead of being alone, they take it better. When a leader takes some of the pain right along with the group, they become a member of the team, not an aloof "boss."

There are many instances when you need to share the pain, for example, when:

- Your group experiences a performance failure or setback.
- People must work late or overtime or weekends to meet crucial deadlines.
- Budgets are cut.
- People need to cover for missing team members.
- Group emergencies arise.

These things happen, but how they are interpreted is another matter. If you roll up your sleeves and get to work shoulder-to- shoulder with the troops or, if you take a pay freeze or pay cut just like everyone else (when you are not required to) – that is sharing the pain. That is what builds genuine respect and "esprit de corps."

Share the Spotlight

The "spotlight" is a reference to any time a compliment or more formal accolade comes your way. You do not work in a vacuum. Give credit to everyone who was meaningfully involved in, or was supportive of your work. If your gratitude is real you will build wonderfully strong relationships.

CHALLENGE:

Next time you receive a glowing employee evaluation or performance review, go thank your peers and others with whom you regularly interact for helping you accomplish your goals.

If you hog the limelight too much your key relationships will sour in a hurry and you just might end up working in a vacuum!

Share the Standards

The "standards" are any rules or policies that apply to employees. When you ask others to do something, you must be prepared to do it yourself. There are exceptions of course, but it is a great general rule to live by. When they see you not conforming to the same standards, you cease being the leader and become "the boss."

RULE 3 – STAY POSITIVE

Your general mental state every day has a profound impact on what you accomplish. It also has a huge influence on those whom you lead and those with whom you interact.

Positivity Matters – A Lot!
Positive emotions come in many shapes and sizes from happiness to gratitude to thankfulness to a positive anticipation and eagerness towards your work. Positive emotions are contagious! Importantly, they can:

- Improve creative thinking
- Reduce defensiveness
- Help people see commonalities
- Improve attitudes
- Relieve stress

While it can be difficult to always stay positive, your challenge is clear:

- **Work to stay positive.** Sometimes it is hard work – but it is worth it. How you view any situation is up to you. Choosing a positive perspective makes your next task – helping others – much easier.

- **Help others stay positive.** This is one of the best gifts you can give anyone. Frankly, if you are a leader, it is your responsibility. It involves three major activities: positively framing issues when you communicate, being supportive and encouraging, and watching out for others on your team.

Positively Framing How You Communicate

Every situation has positive possibilities. How you frame a message or task influences how it is received. For example, say you need the team to stay late to finish a task for a key client. Is this a need to stay late (negative frame) or an opportunity to secure a long-term client (positive frame)?

On average, if you create and use the positive frame, your team will:

- Feel motivated instead of burdened
- Persevere more in the face of challenge
- Explore new outside-the-box possibilities
- Espouse a higher belief in the work

Be Supportive and Encouraging

Positivity, supportiveness, and encouragement are probably the cheapest and most effective tools in your arsenal. Why is it so hard to understand the power of encouragement?

It is not cliché, it is true – leaders are supposed to be cheerleaders. Cheerleaders both applaud and console. They applaud both specific and general team efforts. That means they yell when the team makes a great play and they also cheer randomly on the sidelines.

The cheerleader reality highlights a great fact: your effort to encourage others does not have to be elaborate or over-the-top to have a positive effect. Try a genuine "thank you" or "nice job" and watch what happens.

CHALLENGE:
Stop assuming your team does not need a pat on the back and go check in with them once in a while.

Cheerleader job #2 is consoling. Even after the team's most tragic loss, the dutiful cheerleader finds time to put an arm around the person who missed the winning shot.

Recognize that any worthy outcome (e.g., a process improvement or new product) results from endless attempts and efforts. Then you will see the clear need to be supportive and encouraging.

Watching Out For Your Peers & Teammates

Your boss walks into your office and informs you that Bob, a member of your team, made a mistake resulting in an upset customer. You are unaware of the issue. What do you do? You have a choice: Cover your butt and hang Bob out to dry, or take up for one of your own.

Sometimes the cheerleading uniform has to get a little dirty. Bob may, or may not have made a good decision, but that is not the point. The point is that if you want to develop others and build positive relationships in your group, you must err towards protecting Bob. Otherwise, the next time you walk by waving your pom-poms he will roll his eyes.

"Keeping it in the family" is important not only for how Bob views you moving forward, but also for how the rest of the team views you. To the extent that you can, shelter Bob from the wrath of someone he does not even report to, and he will move mountains on your behalf in the future – and so will the rest of the team.

4

MOTIVATING AND DEVELOPING OTHERS

ADDRESSING PERFORMANCE ISSUES

A performance deviation may be on the soft side or the hard side. The soft side deals with personality, attitude, communication, or other soft skills. The hard side deals with the actual work tasks to be accomplished.

When you become aware of a performance issue ask the following two questions:

- Is the issue simply bothersome and irritating, or is it hurting morale or productivity?

- Am I looking at a discrete incident or is this a pattern?

If you are dealing with a mildly irksome incident as opposed to a pattern of behavior that is negatively impacting morale and productivity, err on little to no intervention. You cannot fix everything, you do not want to micromanage, and you need to save your ammunition for the bigger fights.

Yes, mere incidents (as opposed to patterns) sometimes require an intervention if they are severe enough. However, the guideline is to target patterns because you have finite time and energy.

Your intervention will consist of an interpersonal interaction designed to understand the deviation and set or clarify expectations. If it is warranted, you might also develop a performance improvement plan. This is a written and mutually agreed upon set of skills to build and /or tasks to accomplish over a specified period of time required to move the person's performance back into an acceptable range.

When in doubt, use feedback, not a performance improvement plan.

To add impact in more serious cases, consider making the feedback formal by having the employee sign a printed copy acknowledging receipt. When you deliver the feedback, check your emotions and follow the guidelines for effective communication noted in Rule 1!

Always remember that when one of your employees has a performance problem, you own the burden of responsibility for addressing the issue (not them).

Get to the Root Cause

Before you deliver the feedback, be absolutely sure that you know what is causing the issue. Anytime you see a performance issue that needs to be addressed, ask yourself whether it is best explained by ability (they need new or stronger skills) or motivation (they need new focus and energy).

Most leaders rush too quickly to judgment one way or the other.

Motivating and Developing Others 71

If you assume ability, but the answer is motivation, you risk alienating the person by offering training and assistance to an adequately skilled person. If you assume motivation and the better answer is ability, you risk misleading a person who actually needs to engage in skill building.

Do not assume you know the answer. For starters, go talk to them and gain their insight. Next, ask yourself:

- How difficult is the work?

- How skilled is the person?

- Are they providing a strong effort?

Generally, if the work is considered difficult within the context of this person's normal role, if the person is not among the most highly skilled on the team, and they have been putting in a high-quality effort – you have an ability problem.

When you face ability problems, there are three major remedies: training, reshaping the role, and releasing the employee.

Training. Training is the most common approach to addressing ability issues. It is a formal short-term effort to build specific targeted skills.

First rule of training:
Training is not a right – it is a privilege.

To determine whether a person requires training, ask yourself:

- Can the skill area in question be reasonably addressed via training?
- Is the person trainable?
- Is the training budget healthy?

If the answer to these questions is basically "yes," training is a viable option.

To ensure you receive maximum value from your training dollars, you must get the right people the right training, at the right time, from the right resource, and then ensure transfer of learning back to the workplace.

- **The right people**. People too often receive training because they are new, since everyone else has, etc. The right people are those with a legitimate need to build skills.

- **At the right time**. The right time is as soon as possible after a need is identified. This is one reason "on-demand" training solutions are growing in popularity.

- **From the right resource**. A great rule: secure the highest quality resource you can afford. If you want a strong return on your training dollars you cannot always use the "value" option in the market.

- **Transfer of learning**. After training is complete, the learner must return to a workplace where the boss and key colleagues are meaningfully supportive of the new skills gained, otherwise you have simply wasted training dollars.

If you fail to correctly address one or more of the issues above, your training budget will not add much value.

CHALLENGE:

For you and your team, think through all of the training classes and events completed over the past 12 months. For what portion did all of the preceding characteristics apply?

Reshape their role. If you believe training is inadequate, you may be facing a significant mismatch between the person's capabilities and their current duties. Consider changing what it is the person does – a little or a lot – to better match what they are capable of doing.

Enlarge or restrict the scope of one or more current responsibilities. Add new responsibilities. Remove some responsibilities. Some combination of these efforts may better align their interests and abilities with their work.

The downside: It takes time to reshape someone's role and time is a precious resource. Also, others might feel you are unfairly helping the person in question. Nonetheless, this is worth a sincere try given the huge cost of turnover.

If this person is removed due to performance, you then face the significant costs associated with recruiting, hiring, training, and socializing a new colleague.

Releasing the person. "Letting them go," or "separating," or "releasing" are all euphemisms for firing someone. Firing is expensive. Do not forget the costs associated with turnover.

There is a right way and a wrong way to fire someone due to significant performance problems.

A person has been removed from their job and/or your organization correctly when all of the following are true:

- Less severe measures were genuinely considered as first options.

- The person was not surprised. The outcome was predictable given the feedback provided over time.

- The formal performance paper trail clearly supports the outcome.

- Multiple documented opportunities were provided to improve by using very specific feedback, goal setting, and clear expectations.

- The interpersonal treatment surrounding the entire process was factual and positive.

- Reasonable efforts were made to assist the person in finding future employment.

- Following the event, the person's removal was explained to relevant others at work factually and positively to ensure the event was understood and does not become fodder for negative rumors.

Believe it or not, firing someone might be the best thing for them. Assuming the decision was a high quality decision (it adhered, at a minimum, to the standards above), you not only did what was best for your organization, but you may have helped the person in question by giving them a much needed " wake-up" call.

Firing someone does not mean you lack compassion.

It means that you are working hard to maximize the value created by the unit you lead instead of simply maximizing the development of every individual.

You must find ways to develop your staff, but it is wholly unreasonable to expend large sums of limited budgets on the lowest performing employees.

For the actual conversation in which you will inform someone they are being fired, be diligent and ensure that you:

- **Plan well.** Know exactly how the meeting will take place. Your goal is to have a very concrete agenda of items and to remain in complete control.

- **Be private.** The actual meeting should take place in absolute privacy to ensure a minimum of unease for all parties concerned.

- **Be brief.** Say the minimum, state the facts clearly, but do not discuss irrelevant material and do not be redundant.

- **Don't negotiate.** This is not a dialogue. There is no chance anything they say will change the outcome. Thus, do not let them think otherwise.

- **Don't do it alone.** For future protection (and possible support and assistance) have the proper human resources, managerial, or legal employee present. No more than one is needed and they should not be the person's direct co-worker.

- **Check your emotions.** Stick to the facts and the outcome, not how you or they feel about the facts and the outcome. Begin calm and remain calm no matter what emotions others might show.

- **Explain the process and benefits.** This includes when to leave the premises, what to return before leaving, severance, insurance, etc.

- **Allow feedback.** After you are finished, it is proper to offer the person an opportunity to provide feedback. Manage the situation and keep it brief, but allow them to share any feedback they wish to share.

- **Close positively.** Thank the person for their time and for the effort they have expended on behalf of the organization. Tell them you wish them well. In general, show respect.

There are other fine points, such as whether to ask them to sign a release (promising not to sue you), whether to offer them a financial incentive to do so (e.g., extended severance), etc. However, these are the basics and the better you complete them, the less likely you will be sued for discrimination or wrongful termination.

Finally, to reduce the chance you must fire someone again, you must attempt to determine how this all happened. Was the hiring process flawed? A bad job description? Poor training? There could be many answers and unless you find them you will spend more time firing people than necessary.

CHALLENGE:
Following every difficult performance discussion or firing, have the team discuss the root cause, or risk experiencing the same thing again.

MOTIVATION IS NOT A MYSTERY

With ability out of the way, we can now focus on how to motivate people. A lot of people think motivation is a black art. This is not true at all. There are many effective low or no cost ways to motivate your people.

A motivated employee is strongly invested in their work and committed to the organization both physically and mentally. They tend to perform well, are engaged in both task and positive social activities, and they tend to be enthusiastic and helpful. Creating motivated and productive employees is not rocket science.

Start by differentiating between motivating employees and developing talent:

- **Motivating employees**. Refers to efforts and activities designed to maximize the output of an individual or group given their current skills.
- **Developing talent**. Refers to tools and activities primarily aimed at building new skills.

MOTIVATING EMPLOYEES

Motivating employees involves two major components: creating high quality interpersonal relationships and creating an effective performance management process.

High Quality Interpersonal Relationships

This refers to what you say and do directly to others in casual daily interactions and in response to their performance. The best explanation of what it means to have "high quality interpersonal relationships" is detailed in Dewett's Rules in Chapter 3.

However, two additional ideas are vital. Both are unique to leadership roles, as opposed to the majority of professional roles which do not involve formal leadership: understanding life in the glass house and the importance of authenticity.

When you are elevated into a position of leadership do not expect people to throw roses at your feet. Do not expect people to bow when you enter the room.

The cliché is true: leaders live in glass houses. Expect others to elevate their scrutiny of you and hold you to new higher standards. People who live in glass houses should not only avoid throwing rocks, but they should also be highly sensitive to the example they set.

The wider your visibility, the more you must provide a positive and productive example because everyone is watching.

Stated differently: What you do matters more than what you say. Your IQ, social intelligence, and integrity are revealed by the things you do at work every day. Everyone is a model, but are you a role model?

Second, realize the power of authenticity. In decades past, the standard prototypical leader could be described with words such as powerful, infallible, decisive, and smart.

Today, we realize this list is incomplete. In addition, the best leaders are "authentic."

Your goal is not only to be successful, but to always strive for authenticity. Only then will you be a role model capable of motivating others.

Success might be defined by a promotion, a raise, a degree, a new client, or a huge bonus. Yet without authenticity, it is success without respect or admiration.

In a leadership context, authenticity involves:

- **Integrity**. High-quality moral character is absolutely crucial. Strong integrity allows people to trust you much more than would be the case if you were merely competent at your job.

- **A service mentality**. Quality professionals seek to assist and build others as much as they try to advance themselves. They hold this view because they believe it is "right" from a moral perspective and because they know that one of the best ways to advance a career is to genuinely help others.

- **Showing your humanity**. To be human is to be imperfect and to experience setbacks. Followers and leaders are human – they make mistakes and have "learning moments" all the time. Showing this reality by occasionally referencing a mistake or lesson learned, increases your credibility as a leader while making you "human" in the eyes of others.

To understand the importance of authenticity, you must appreciate the relationship between reverence and fear. To be revered is to be loved and to be shown deferential honor. Sounds great, but there is a catch. When someone is revered at work, the behavioral reaction to them strangely resembles what you would expect to see in the case that they were feared instead of revered.

When you sit high on a pedestal, people censor around you, choose not to offer feedback, and stop questioning you – they blindly follow. Authenticity removes the pedestal and makes you a member of the team, learning and growing along with everyone else.

You do not have to be perfect so long as you are authentic.

Using the Performance Management Process

The interpersonal component is the more informal route towards motivating others. The formal process of motivating others is often referred to as the "performance management process." This involves the systematic use of goals and metrics, evaluations and feedback, recognition and rewards, and accountability.

It has been said that a happy worker is a productive worker. Not true. A happy worker is only productive when they are naturally motivated or when a decent performance management process is in place.

Goals and Metrics

Goals were discussed as they apply to your personal professional development earlier. I stated that useful goals are SMART (specific, measurable, aligned, reachable, and time bound). However, when a leader is involved in setting goals for others, two additional criteria are necessary. The full acronym is now SMART + PR:

- **P is for Participation**. There are times you need to solicit employee input – give them a "voice." Goal setting is one common example. The more they feel they contributed to creating their goals, the more committed they will become.

- **R is for Resources**. If you ask for a certain level of performance, you must provide people the tools required to be successful. They may need new tools, a new budget, new training, etc. Be sure the goals you set are backed up with the proper resources or goals will become demotivational quickly.

Metrics were briefly alluded to in the "M" part of SMART goals – goals must be measurable. When you measure something to gauge progress it is often called a metric. This is a numerical indicator of progress towards your goal. One goal may have more than one metric.

CHALLENGE:
Strive for the bare minimum number of metrics needed to adequately measure performance.

Evaluations and Feedback

The employee evaluation process in most organizations hurts morale and productivity when, in fact, the goal is to boost both. The system is supposed to provide feedback to help employees understand and improve their performance.

Most employee evaluations are administered once or twice per year, and are delivered by people untrained in providing performance-related feedback. Not surprisingly, organizations spend a massive amount of time and money systematically undermining employee motivation as a result.

I am not suggesting that you stop using formal evaluations, but:

- **They should be radically simplified**. A decent evaluation process does not require expensive and cumbersome software programs. For all but the largest of firms, very simple software or paper will suffice. The average number of hours dedicated to this process in most organizations should be cut in half.

- **They should be divorced from the discussion of money**. Many organizations end each performance evaluation session with an employee by discussing compensation-related issues. Not surprisingly, the employees are not engaged at all. They are waiting to hear about raises or bonuses. Effective evaluations are not about money – they are about performance.

- **They should be administered by trained personnel**. Typically anyone with direct reports delivers the evaluation. It is common for this person to have no honest idea how best to discuss all of the performance-related issues to be addressed. Quality training focused on the core ideas in this book provide the foundation.

CHALLENGE:

As part of the next employee survey at work, find out what everyone thinks about the evaluation process and then revisit the costs associated with each cycle to assess where you stand as an organization.

If an employee is surprised by an evaluation, the blame goes to the leader administering the evaluation or providing the feedback. This point reveals the most important approach to evaluating performance:

Quality performance management is not about infrequent formal discussions. It is all about frequent informal discussions.

Frequent informal performance-related chats are the perfect forum for you to deliver needed feedback to your employees. Great feedback has the following characteristics:

- **It abides by the rules of effective communication**. (Honest, specific, concise, supportive, timely) For performance feedback, "timely" may be the most crucial. The less timely you are, the less likely your target will fully understand what you are trying to communicate.

- **It offers help, not mere criticism**. Understand that people do not like being "evaluated." They will, however, respect being "helped." Your goal is to offer a useful idea, resource, or helping hand for every critical comment you specify.

- **It is offered in the right amount**. Every person and bit of feedback represents a unique combination. You do not want to give people more than they can process effectively. If you overload them, you have not helped them – you have made things worse. Start small and go deeper as you determine it is safe and productive to do so.

- **It is about outcomes and behaviors, not people and their shortcomings**. Focus on the easy to digest objects: the actual work products in question and the objective behaviors you have witnessed leading to the production of the work products. Do not get personal unless it is unavoidable. The more you focus on the objective work instead of your subjective view of the individual, the more likely they will take your feedback seriously.

- **It involves the receiver's response and confirmation**. Good feedback is not a lecture, but a discussion you control. Importantly, the discussion is not over until you have confirmation that the recipient understands what you were trying to say. Do not simply ask them what they heard. Try having them repeat back to you a very quick summary.

- **It is clearly connected to outcomes and consequences**. The receiver deserves to understand how the feedback relates to outcomes of interest. What are the key processes, services, or products that are eventually influenced by the performance issue at hand? Next, if necessary, the receiver must know what possible consequences lay ahead if performance does not change (for themselves and/or the group).

- **It is framed positively**. This means two things: First, it includes affirming feedback, not merely critical feedback. Second, it frames the critical feedback as opportunities, not as shortcomings. Take the positive route.

If your organization wishes to dramatically increase collective performance, invest less in time consuming and onerous formal evaluation processes.

Ironically, many organizations spend an inordinate proportion of their training and development dollars on technical skills and advanced interpersonal skills, all of which are dependent on basic people skills that are lacking.

CHALLENGE:
Spend more on basic training designed to create more thoughtful and productive communicators.

Only then will you see more informal, frequent, positive, and candor-filled performance-related discussions.

Avoid Micro-Managing

Though you need to give feedback, you must avoid "micro-managing." This refers to an overbearing or incessant need to control the smallest of tasks addressed by your team.

People sometimes micro-manage because:

- They like control.

- They do not trust others.

- They believe they have better skills.

A great rule of thumb is to manage outcomes, not processes.

Translated: give employees reasonable autonomy and only dive deep in the process details when the outcomes they produce do not meet required standards.

RECOGNITION AND REWARDS

To effectively recognize great efforts and reward great achievements you must appreciate the difference between intrinsic motivation and extrinsic motivation.

After that, the remaining guidelines are simple: err on using non-monetary efforts more than monetary efforts, ensure that all recognition and rewards are provided contingent on performance, and make sure your efforts treat people as unique individuals.

Intrinsic Versus Extrinsic Motivation

Intrinsic motivation is a fancy way to say that someone is motivated to do something because, to some meaningful degree, they like it – they enjoy what they do, they are a good "fit" with their role, and they are naturally inclined to feel positively about their job.

Intrinsic motivation comes from two major sources. The first, which you cannot change, is the person's personality and genes. Some people are simply a better "fit" with some roles than others.

The second, which is as big, or bigger than the first, is under your control: a positive and transparent work environment. One major hurdle to developing and unleashing intrinsic motivation is the array of external forces at play. Call them "extrinsic motivators." That refers to money in your paycheck, your bonus check, the informal rewards you receive, punishments, the time clock you have to punch – all of the external structures and incentives that influence you at work.

Here is a summary of a few thousand studies on motivation: intrinsic motivation is stupendous (for morale, productivity, creativity) and we have to find ways to build it; extrinsic motivation is good so long as it does not mess up intrinsic motivation.

Consider what typically happens at work. Well-intentioned leaders go too far creating structures, tricks, and gimmicks to cajole others into performing. The main culprit, predictably, tends to be an unduly strong focus on money as a motivator.

The Importance of Non-Monetary Motivators

Money does not matter nearly as much as you think it does. At home or work, no amount of money replaces great relationships.

Leaders generally like money more than the folks whom they lead. The fact that money motivates leaders more is not a bad thing per se. The problem is that leaders too often assume that money is a prime motivator for others.

Employees, of course, do like money and want to continue receiving their paychecks. Yet, when you go ask them what really makes them happy, they will say things like being appreciated, being in the loop, and having good relationships.

Money is rarely near the top of the list.

If you want more bang for your buck, you actually have to stop spending so many bucks.

There are many potentially useful monetary motivators that serve as a financial "thank you," such as a day of paid vacation, tickets to a sporting event, gift certificates of any form, simple cash payouts, and more elaborate efforts such as gain sharing.

Gain sharing deserves special attention because it represents the best and the worst of the monetary approaches to motivation.

Gain sharing involves measuring some aspect of performance over time. When a group or unit performs above some historical standard, that is a "gain," and it is financially quantified and shared with the workers according to some agreed upon formula.

Unfortunately, this often leads to myopic views of the organization, employees questioning management decisions based on how it affects parameters in the formula, and in general, moves the employees' focus from the work to the formula.

If you overindulge in monetary approaches to motivation – whether it is gift certificates or gain sharing, the following ugly outcomes are likely:

- **People begin to expect more monetary rewards.** They never expect less, always more, always bigger.

- **People feel left out.** If someone does not receive a reward, even if they do not honestly deserve a reward, they often feel resentment.

- **Your thinking becomes less productive.** As a leader, you stop thinking about people and processes and begin instead thinking about new possible rewards that will motivate your employees.

- **Employees stop thinking as much about the work.** The more financial motivators are present, the more they become the focus instead of the work.

Monetary motivators are not improper. They simply cannot be your major approach to motivating others. If you do use them, make sure:

- **The performance in question is amazing.** The instance of performance being rewarded cannot be average or a little better than average. It must be spectacular.

- **You provide a great public explanation.** This helps others understand the nature of the rewarded performance, thereby setting expectations as to the level of performance required to be so honored.

- **You provide the reward immediately.** The time when the reward is viewed as most justified and when it is most understood by all observers is immediately following performance, not weeks or months later. Periodic, formal ceremonies can be nice, but do not lose your opportunity to motivate, "in the moment."

Not only are non-monetary motivators free or cheap compared to financially-oriented rewards, but there are many more of them. Imagine the unlimited versions of these common examples:

- **Recognition for their work**. A pat on the back, "job well done," "congratulations," "great work," etc. Public or private, to an individual or group – genuine positive comments are terribly useful.

The two most important words in business are, "Thank you."

- **Recognition concerning work efforts**. This is a neglected tactic. Great outcomes only materialize once in a while. In the meantime, thanking people for their efforts is invaluable. Do not drown them in praise, but do not forget to recognize the efforts and the outcomes.

- **Non-financial benefits or perks**. These refer to non-monetary (though not cost free) efforts to support quality work-life balance such as: flex-time, in-house valet services, or health club memberships.

- **Awards**. Awards are a physical reminder of a particular achievement. Common awards involve certificates, plaques, or any number of other objects deemed to represent the achievement symbolically.

- **Celebratory ceremonies**. Ceremonies are the actual events surrounding the delivery of awards. When creative and thoughtful, they can be as meaningful as the award itself.

- **Provide autonomy**. One of the greatest rewards is to be treated like a capable professional. When provided with reasonable liberty at work, employees feel much stronger ownership over their work.

- **Connect to the outcomes**. Give employees purpose while saying thank you: if they work to support a much larger process or some far away final product or service, help them understand their contribution. Use pictures, videos, or share a customer "thank-you" letter with the entire group.

Contingent on Performance

There are thousands of ways to recognize and reward your employees. The problem is not finding ways to say thank you.

The problem is that we usually recognize and reward people too much.

Since we all recognize the importance of the basic notion of motivation, it is easy to over recognize. We send out emails touting others' successes, we select the employee of the month, we have quarterly recognition ceremonies with food or gifts.

The profound rule we too often neglect is that all recognition and rewards should be provided contingent on performance.

Not for showing up. Not for average performance either, but for providing clearly above average efforts and for achieving clearly above average outcomes.

CHALLENGE:

Do a quick count in your head. How many people in your office have received that certificate from the office laser printer that says, "High 5 Award," or "Super Achiever," or "Team Player?"

If you have trouble naming the people who have not yet received the award, you know exactly what I mean.

Under such conditions, the award will soon cease to have any positive effect. In fact, it can have a negative effect. Rewarding people because they are mediocre or because they simply meet standards is bad practice.

When you reward mediocrity, you get more of it – and you really upset your high performers.

At work we have, "A players" (by far the most capable employees; usually about 20% of the employee base), "B players" (the worthy and reliable 70% of most organizations), and "C players" (the underperformers who snuck through the cracks in your hiring process; about 10%).

Treating B players like A players makes the B players think they are A players. They quickly grow an entitlement mentality. The A players rightly feel underappreciated and either 1) stop trying so hard, or 2) leave the organization.

Treating C players like B players by making sure they all eventually receive the quarterly High Five award is a sure way to kill the morale of all of your A and B players.

Leaders must reward and recognize people legitimately based on performance and by maintaining a positive and transparent work environment.

People Are Unique Individuals

When you recognize the correct people at the right time, give serious consideration to making the awards individualized. When every past recipient has an identical award, it can lose its meaning.

People are individuals and appreciate being recognized as such.

The more personal, tailored and idiosyncratic the reward, the more it looks, feels, and operates like a support for intrinsic motivation. Even for formal awards that are given out at regular intervals, you can make them personal and try to ensure they support intrinsic motivation.

Underneath the part that says, "Outstanding Service Achievement," put something novel in parentheses like, "For putting up with Herb when no one else could." Find the low cost way to personally say thank you for the specific achievement being honored.

CHALLENGE:

Again, write down the major rewards handed out where you work and note which ones are regularly awarded contingent on performance and which ones are also personalized.

Accountability

Here is the last piece of the performance management process: accountability. You hold people accountable when you give them the feedback and outcomes they deserve given their performance, relative to whatever goals and standards are in effect.

This is easy when people meet or exceed standards and much harder when they do not. Thus, many people fail to properly hold others accountable. Leaders sometimes fail to hold people accountable because:

- **They do not like conflict.** Generally, people do not enjoy giving negative or critical feedback. So, they skip it or water it down – and performance suffers.

- **They are not being held accountable themselves.** It is tough to hold others to meaningful standards when you are not being evaluated in a similar fashion.

- **They see other leaders not holding people accountable.** When there is wide variance in the consistency of application of the performance management process, some feel pressure to ease up simply because that is what others are doing.

This is particularly sad in organizations that spend good money on the other parts of the performance management system. Without accountability, half or more of the dollars spent on the other parts of the system are being wasted.

Why would you expect goals to work when there is no accountability?

Holding your team accountable is not always easy, but you can do it if you:

- **Fall in love with Dewett's Rules**. Seriously, this is the foundation for everything else.

- **Set clear goals and standards**. Use public visual goal tracking where applicable to maximize performance visibility.

- **Specify consequences**. It is not enough to set great goals. They only work if people understand that persistent poor performance is not supported.

- **Hold yourself to the standards**. When your team sees you behaving and performing in a manner consistent with what you have asked of them you are seen as legitimate.

- **Keep your eye on morale**. As you become better at holding people accountable, do not neglect all of the important soft-side issues that support strong morale.

- **Are consistent**. Nothing sinks a performance management process faster than the perception that it is applied to some people strictly, others moderately, and to others not at all. Use it consistently.

- **Provide great feedback**. Informally, between evaluations and during the formal sit downs, remember the characteristics of good feedback noted earlier: it abides by the rules of effective communication, offers help, in the right amount, about outcomes and behaviors – not people, involves the receiver's response and confirmation, is clearly connected to outcomes and consequences, and is framed positively.

Group Rewards

A minority of the tangible rewards you use need to be group rewards. A group reward is one received by every member of the team when an agreed upon performance goal is reached, otherwise it is given to no member of the team. If group members wish to receive a performance-contingent reward, they have a vested interest in their teammates' performance.

The performance goal might concern attendance, an amount of work to be completed, meeting a deadline, a level of quality achieved, an amount of sales generated, time saved, or many others. When the reward is valued by most group members, they will voluntarily work to support positive performance in others and will confront negative performance issues promptly. In short, when they share a possible reward, teams begin to self-correct.

DEVELOPING TALENT

Motivation is about maximizing the value added of current skills. Developing talent – often referred to as leadership development – is about future skills.

The major vehicles used to develop talent include: skill assessments, shadowing and rotations, training or seminars, self-directed study, delegating, stretch goals and assignments, mentoring, coaching, and formal educational degrees.

There is no perfect mix of these activities. The main point is that if you use these tools, you need to use them correctly.

Used incorrectly, they can actually cause harm!

Skill Assessments

Assessments are tools used to evaluate the current state of a particular skill or skills a person possesses. The tools might be simple and low cost, such as self-administered survey instruments, or complex and expensive, such as dedicated assessment centers.

Assessment centers staffed by highly competent personnel are wonderful, though only large organizations can afford them. Dedicated and highly-trained personnel observe employees as they engage in a variety of individual and group tasks.

For most professionals, assessment will consist of surveys and tests, work-based assessments, and observation and evaluation by relevant experts.

Surveys and tests. There are many available on the market to assess virtually any skill area, hard or soft. The key is to be sure you purchase a validated tool. There are many low cost and highly questionable tools available. Whether you go the paper route, computer-based, or some form of online administration, do the homework to vet the resource.

Work-based assessments. A simple on-the-job method of assessing skills is to give a person an actual task to work on while being observed by a relevant expert. Every job is different – it might involve using a type of software, using a tool or machine, conducting an analysis, etc.

Observation and evaluation. This involves on-the-job observation of an employee, assuming you have staff dedicated to professional development. If not, the most common method of giving feedback for development purposes is 360° feedback programs.

The idea for 360° programs is simple: gather relevant performance-related feedback (hard and soft) for a person from their direct supervisor(s), relevant peers, and their direct reports. The feedback is collected in all directions.

When the culture supports honesty and candor and/or when participants believe participation is confidential and anonymous, 360° programs can be very useful.

Caveat: far too often they are applied to people who do not want feedback. In such cases you are wasting money and adding no value.

Shadowing and Rotations

Both are methods of expanding an employee's skill base. Shadowing is a low- risk method that entails one employee following a highly-competent employee for a period of time to learn by observation. The only downside is the lack of productivity for the follower during the time they are not actually working.

Job rotations are a more expansive option. The idea is to help the person understand more slices of the organizational pie – to see part-whole relationships more strategically. Instead of shadowing, they actually take on completely new roles and responsibilities.

Rotation programs are sometimes used for younger high-potential employees who are moved through different functional positions in a predetermined manner over the course of multiple years.

They can also be used within a unit to help key individuals learn all major tasks/processes in the unit over time. When used this way, they provide a great hedge against turnover and absences.

Training and Seminars

Training was addressed earlier in response to an ability-related performance problem.

You must give the right people the right training, at the right time, from the right resource, and then ensure transfer of learning back to the workplace.

Training is also a common and useful tool for building new skills. For either soft-side or hard-side training, one of the first issues you face is whether to use internal talent or external talent.

Using internal talent to deliver training offers:

- **Familiarity with the business**. If they are in the business, they have deep knowledge about how concepts addressed in training apply to the work learners actually do every day.

- **Content control**. Topically, what you want is delivered. Internal resources make it easier to align training with the organization's mission, vision, and objectives.

- **Cost control**. High-quality internal resources typically cost less compared to high-quality external resources.

Using external talent to deliver training offers:

- **Fresh perspectives**. External resources do not say, "It can't be done," or "That will not work because…"They are wonderfully naïve about your inner workings and thus see and stimulate new perspectives.
- **No fear of sacred cows**. As opposed to internal resources who may censor, the external resource is blissfully unaware of any sacred cows. Further, if identified, they are more willing to talk about them, which is rare with internal trainers.
- **Skills not possessed by internal candidates**. You can go to the market and find anything you do not have internally. External experts provide instant bench strength.
- **Access to best practices**. Though there are other sources (e.g., books, conferences), using outside talent is often a great vehicle for learning best practices for both the hard-side and soft-side issues.

Self-Directed Study

As computer technologies continue to advance in capability, and drop in price, self-paced digital learning options have proliferated. There are many paper-based options available as well. In either case, there are pros and cons to self-directed learning.

The pros include:

- **Flexibility and convenience**. This benefits users immensely since they can be engaged on multiple devices when computer-based, and during work hours or after whether the tool is paper or digital.

- **Low cost per user**. Especially for digital options, over time as these tools are used by increasing numbers of employees, the cost per employee is reasonable.

- **Consistent standard**. Standardized tools (digital or not) provide a reliable benchmark for assessing large numbers of employees over time.

- **Great for hard-side skills**. Digital tools in particular are useful for learning technical or complex skills. Given the lack of interpersonal activity, self-directed learning options are not as well suited for soft skills (though they are often used).

There are also important cons to self-directed learning:

- **Insufficient application**. No computer-based training perfectly mimics reality. For example, a live "role play" trumps an online scenario with questions anytime. Nothing replaces learning in the actual target context.

- **More difficult to tailor to individual needs**. Most self-directed learning products are standard products, thus "fit" with the ability and learning style of any given learner will vary.

- **Often used as a weak checkmark**. Sometimes these tools allow many "do overs" until the learner, in essence, clicks the right box. If everyone always passes the test, has the tool helped people build skills or helped the organization differentiate performers at all?

Delegating

Delegating is entrusting someone to complete a task or project that is normally outside of their job duties, yet is still related to their current skill set. It is the most common simple method of developing others.

How do you know it is time to start delegating more as a leader? Consider delegating as an option when:

- **You see a willing and able employee.** The classic first answer is that you have actively looked for and found a person who desires to grow and for whom you have applicable new work.

- **Employee turnover and apathy are too high**. If your employees sense no room to grow and become bored or jaded, their performance suffers and they are more likely to leave if possible.

- **External constituents only know you**. If you are working too many hours because most external constituents (e.g., suppliers, customers) only work with you and not your team – consider delegating.

- **Your personal performance is suffering**. If you have started missing deadlines or have begun questioning the quality of your own work, it may be because you are personally stretched so thin and are trying to control too much.

- **Employee commitment is crucial**. When this is true (e.g., working on a new vacation policy), and time is available, consider not only soliciting input, but also try delegating some portion of the task.

Delegating is typically enacted incorrectly. To get the most out of your delegation efforts, be sure that you:

- **Delegate at the right time**. The wrong time is when you are so busy you feel compelled to offload some of your work onto a subordinate. If you do that, people will know you have merely used delegation as a time management strategy – not good. The right time is when you have a good task/project that will actually help a subordinate build new skills.

- **Delegate to the right person**. Everyone does not want to be delegated to and not everyone is ready for expanded roles. The right person is ready (has good potential) and willing (motivated to grow).

- **Delegate the right work**. Do not delegate busy work, undesirable work, or boring work. Always attempt to delegate work that will be meaningful to the person.

- **Delegate the right amount**. Assuming you have the right person, delegate an amount they can handle, which differs per person. Too much or too little and you can actually demotivate. Consult with them to determine the correct amount.

- **Allow participation**. To get the type and scope of work correct, have a meaningful dialogue. Do not make a delegation decision without their input or it will likely be viewed as an autocratic mandate, not a developmental opportunity.

- **Provide responsibility, authority, and resources**. If you give the responsibility, you also have to give the needed authority to act, and any needed resources. In short, give them all the tools they need to be successful.

- **Do not allow reverse delegation**. For whatever reason, if the person attempts to delegate the task back to you, do not allow it. Correct any implementation errors, but let them own the work. Otherwise, you increase the risk of future reverse delegation.

- **Do not micro-manage.** Many professionals have trouble letting go. If you delegate, check up periodically, but let them do the work free from your prying eyes. As noted earlier, micro-managing signals to your employee that you simply do not trust them.

- **Provide clear explanations**. Make sure: 1) they know you are delegating because you believe in them and want to build new skills, and 2) that your expectations for the work are crystal clear. Do not assume they understand either of these – talk about it and be sure.

- **Provide useful feedback**. As their performance unfolds, there will be "bumps in the road" – moments when performance does not look good. This is normal.

Provide positive and helpful feedback to keep them on track. Find the sweet spot between 100% autonomy and micro-managing that works for both of you.

Stretch Goals and Assignments

We have addressed goals for your professional development and goals you set for your subordinates. One final perspective is required. We must consider an important exception to the SMART guidelines noted earlier. Usually, the "R" for Reachable is very justified. However, over the long-term, you need at least one BHAG.

BHAG: Big Hairy Audacious Goal.

The logic is simple. You need to occasionally dream big, think big, and set big goals – because if you do not strive for amazing outcomes you will not achieve amazing outcomes. BHAGs, or "stretch goals," are vital to maximizing your performance.

Yes, they are risky when compared to "Reachable" goals. However – no risk, no reward. You know you have found a possible BHAG when envisioning achieving it makes you smile broadly, and yet you cringe when thinking about the work it will take to get there. BHAGs ask you to push your current skills to new levels, while building new skills.

Consider the following comparison of goals and BHAGs:

- Goal: reduce production set-up time by at least 10%. BHAG: reduce production set-up time by over 90%.

- Goal: produce competent leaders. BHAG: produce leaders capable of reinventing the organization.

- Goal: push to market at least five new products next fiscal year. BHAG: create a new market using an entirely new business model.

Remember, anything worth having does not come easy.

If you do use BHAGs, keep these guidelines in mind:

- For you or your team, 1 or 2 every few years will suffice (BHAGS take great energy and resources)
- "Go public" with your close confidants and discuss the desired outcome often (the more you discuss the dream, the more real it becomes)
- If you help create a BHAG for someone else, be helpful (BHAGs are difficult), patient (they take time), and forgiving (it is normal to fall short when pursuing a BHAG)

CHALLENGE:
Can you articulate at least one personal BHAG and one team BHAG?

A stretch assignment differs from a stretch goal. A stretch goal is a very tough goal within your current area of responsibility. A stretch assignment involves duties and goals in new areas of responsibility.

Mentoring

A mentoring relationship is a strategic skill-building relationship focused on long-term career development within the organization and/or vocation.

Mentoring is about providing advice, insight, and potential access to new network contacts. Your mentor can be a member of your organization or not, with similar implications as discussed with regard to internal versus external trainers.

Mentoring programs at work often pair a junior person with a senior person so the less experienced employee might learn about career paths, career strategies, organizational history, and other institutional knowledge. Another key goal is to enlarge the junior employee's professional network.

To maximize their effectiveness, mentoring programs should:

- **Be organic and voluntary**. Contrived relationships are not terribly useful. The best mentoring relationships are established naturally, not assigned by mandate.

- **Be supported**. Some nominal amount of time and money should be allocated to allow the mentor and mentee to meet. Further, though mandates are not ideal, leadership must espouse the value of establishing mentor relationships – and make themselves available as mentors.

- **Involve people not directly linked**. Though it is possible your boss could be your mentor, it is not ideal. The required confidentiality and freedom to speak about career-related issues suggests that the mentee should not directly report to the mentor.

- **Be time bound**. Some agree with this, some do not. The idea is that finite time provides an incentive to act constructively and proactively. It also allows a socially acceptable end to the relationship if needed. Having said that – if you are lucky enough to find a really good mentor, hang on to them!

Here are a few things to keep in mind about mentors. They should:

- **Avoid self-biased assumptions**. Recall that this is when you think they think like you think about an issue – or that they really should think like you think. Just because you love golf does not mean your mentee must love golf.

- **Listen**. If you want to actually help them, listen more than you talk. As a result, you will learn more about them and be better positioned to offer useful advice and counsel.

- **Tell it like it is**. Assuming confidentiality is in place, call it like you see it. Try not to sugarcoat the feedback you provide. Be positive – but honest.

- **Be vetted**. For formal mentoring programs, there needs to be some honest consideration given to who serves as a mentor. Just because someone wishes to be a mentor does not mean they should be a mentor.

In an advisory capacity, some people can do more harm than good.

Similarly, there are a few things to keep in mind about mentees. They should:

- **Be respectful of the mentor's time**. Remember, if they are worth being your mentor, they are extremely busy people. Be on time!

- **Show honest gratitude**. No need to, "kiss butt," but do make a genuine statement about how much you appreciate their support and assistance.

- **Look for ways to help in return**. They might need your assistance on a project, access to a member of your network, etc. Look for the possibilities.

- **Stay in touch**. A good mentor will want to know how you grow and develop. Keep them in the loop as your career progresses. In addition, you will remain someone they may think of as professional opportunities arise.

Coaching

A coaching relationship is a tactical skill-building relationship focused on short-term performance improvement.

Like mentors, coaches can be a part of your organization or not. Aside from the short-term versus long-term difference, coaching differs from mentoring in that a mentor is typically significantly removed in the hierarchy from the mentee whereas a coach is often directly connected to the person being coached. It could be one's direct supervisor or a close peer.

Whereas a mentor might discuss long-term career moves, a coach is focused on short-term accomplishments. The targets can be hard or soft skills, but the focus is on creating goals over one or two performance periods (not years) targeted at a very specific set of skills.

In addition, coaches must:

- **Communicate often**. The closer hierarchical relationship of a coach (versus a mentor) and the shorter-term nature of the goals to be achieved necessitate frequent communication.

- **Ask great questions**. Coaches often have the desire to quickly offer advice. While that can be useful, when time allows, it is best to begin with great questions. Ideally, a coach guides the person being coached towards finding answers on their own.

- **Make the relationship mutual**. One excellent way to help the recipient engage the coaching process is for the coach to not only offer help and guidance, but to solicit professional feedback for themselves as well when appropriate.

- **Make goals very focused**. Goals should be very finite, specified, concrete, and measureable. You are essentially trying to help the person form new habits. Goals have the greatest effect when they focus on specific behaviors.

All coaching relationships are unique. Depending on the nature of the two people involved and the nature of the particular performance context, the specific goals pursued will vary.

As you try to judge yourself as a coach and the role of coaching within the performance culture where you work, keep in mind:

- **Not everyone wants to be coached**. Some people resent coaching. The reasons vary. Do not begin the coaching dialogue seeking to understand how to coach a particular person. Begin by seeking to understand whether they truly wish to be coached.

- **Not everyone is coachable**. Some people do not have a personality conducive to a coaching (or mentoring) relationship. They simply learn better and more comfortably via alternative mechanisms. Of course, anyone who does not value performance improvement is not a good candidate for coaching.

- **Not everyone should be coached**. You have a finite amount of time and energy to spend on developing others. Choose your targets wisely. You are looking for the employees who are most receptive and have the highest potential. You cannot coach everyone.

- **Some coaches need to retire**. There is no shortage of people who want to be coaches, who nonetheless lack the interpersonal savvy to be good coaches. They might do some good, but overall cause too much damage. If they report to you, sometimes you need to tell them to retire (as coaches, not as valued employees).

Education Degrees

Formal education degrees can represent high quality, though also high cost, development options. To ensure that the large amount of time and money used provide a solid return, consider the following:

- **Degree type**. For many, the MBA degree and the EMBA degree are solid choices. Other niche degrees should be chosen with caution only when the person has a burning desire for the area and it clearly aligns with their career goals (and organizational needs if the company is paying).

- **High quality above all else**. This refers to the quality of instruction and the quality of the network you will become a part of having attended a particular college or university. Convenience and cost are nice considerations, but quality trumps both.

- **Err on face-to-face**. This is an aspect of the quality issue. The massive growth of on-line and low-residence hybrid programs speaks to a demand for convenience among busy working professionals. The online models have merit, but nothing aids learning and networking as well as live face-to-face interactions and collaborations.

- **Application to individual jobs and industries**. Better programs will allow elements of the coursework to be applied to the student's company, role, and industry. This increases transfer of learning and boosts the educational return on investment.

- **Human Resource policy**. Some companies have no policy and make "ad hoc" decisions about covering some, or all of the employee's educational expenses. Others have elaborate policies. If a significant proportion of the employees you supported quickly leave the organization after completing their degrees, you may or may not need a policy, but you definitely need a more attractive work environment!

What is the Right Allocation?

There are many common ways to develop others. If it is true that you can roughly classify employees as "A" players (the top 20%), "B" players (the middle 70%), and "C" players (the bottom 10% of performers), what is a reasonable allocation of your development-related time and money as a leader and as a leadership team?

Many people feel this is a difficult question. It is not. You have a limited budget and limited time. Ask where you will get the greatest bang for your buck.

CHALLENGE:
Realize that the goal is for you to make decisions that maximize the value added to the organization, not to maximize the development of every single employee.

A reasonable approach is to allocate 50% of your development-related time and money towards your A players, 40% for your B players, and 10% for the C players.

Increasing the performance of an A player by one percent adds significantly more value to the organization than increasing the performance of a B player by one percent due to the higher level of ability possessed by A players.

Similarly, a one percent increase in the performance of a B player dwarfs the value added of a one percent increase in the performance of a C player. From this perspective, it is tough to justify investing in C players beyond required compliance-related training, new employee training, safety-related training, or other nominal investments.

Securing the Future
Two additional sets of activities are specifically designed to ensure a good flow of high-quality future leaders for the organization: high-potential programs and succession planning.

High-Potential Programs

At smaller organizations, stretch goals and roles might suffice, yet for larger organizations a more formal approach is warranted.

High-potential employees are identified by their amazing performance and track record. Sometimes people are hired by an organization and later they become identified as a high-potential employee. Others are hired in and placed immediately into a high-potential program.

This class of employees is believed to be so capable they are "tagged" as likely future members of the leadership team. Once identified, they typically progress through a heightened career improvement plan involving functional rotations and various types of training designed to ensure they stay on the path towards leadership positions in the organization. High-potential programs support a healthy pipeline of leadership talent.

The finer details associated with selecting high-potentials and designing their paths is beyond this book. Here, I merely wish to impress upon the reader that it is the responsibility of senior leaders to build future leadership capacity.

CHALLENGE:

Have an open discussion with your leadership team and ask whether or not you are proactively creating a robust leadership pipeline.

The complement to high-potential programs is succession planning. This involves a systematic examination of key leadership roles and the need for future leadership roles. In short, there is a current set of players and you must match the high-potentials with openings (and needed new positions) as they materialize in a manner consistent with organizational strategy.

Succession planning strives to ensure that the organization's current operations are seamlessly continued following leadership turnover. Typical metrics for measuring succession planning success are the percentage of leadership roles filled internally, diversity-related metrics, retention/attrition rates, and the percent of leadership roles with identified successors.

5

PROBLEM SOLVING
& DECISION MAKING 101

PROBLEM SOLVING
VERSUS DECISION MAKING

Problems are discrete challenges we must address – or we think we must address, both big and small. Decisions represent specific points in time during the problem-solving process when you must choose a path forward among multiple possibilities.

Problem solving and decision making are complementary, not synonymous.

Problem solving is a process of addressing particular challenges. Decisions are made to help the problem-solving process flow effectively from beginning to end. Decisions are made by using any one or more, or many, available decision-making tools.

For example, the team has an opportunity to hire a new member. You collect a huge pile of applications, but to move past the big stack towards a short stack, you must make one or more decisions about what you are looking for in a new team member. One or more decision criteria or tools help you get past the decision point and into the next part of the process.

The same logic applies whether discussing hiring, fixing quality problems, addressing vendor issues, or any other problem one might face at work.

Decision-making tools facilitate movement through a problem-solving process.

A SIMPLE
PROBLEM-SOLVING PROCESS

Before stepping through the world's most simple problem-solving process, you need to make a mental commitment. Realize that problems represent opportunities! They are opportunities to:

- Demonstrate competence

- Apply creativity

- Make work-life better

- Improve product/service/process quality

- Help and develop others

- Improve relationships

- Enhance or build new skills

You can view problems in a negative light as onerous, headache-inducing obstacles, or you can choose to see them as interesting opportunities. The positive frame drastically increases the odds of successful problem solving.

Use an Agreed Upon Model

You and your team need an agreed upon place to start. Call it what you like: an approach, methodology, template, or process. It is a mutually agreed upon way you and your team will systematically address the problem at hand.

Assumption: you have time available to use a systematic approach to problem solving.

Sometimes you do, sometimes you do not. We will talk about using the "head" (i.e., a systematic approach) versus the "gut" (i.e., a quick intuitive approach) shortly – for now we will assume you have some time. However, even if you have time, far too often professionals at work do not have an agreed upon problem-solving process.

CHALLENGE:

Where you work, do you know the location of a problem-solving model that can be used for nearly any problem faced by you and your team?

They might have a very specific process for ensuring the quality of a particular process, a huge diagram for new product development, some flow chart for vendor evaluation, etc. – but no generic problem- solving process ready for everyday use.

The DIE model: Define, Investigate, Execute

What is it we want to accomplish with problem solving? We wish to find useful solutions. More crudely stated, we want to kill the problems – make them die.

Step one is to Define the problem. This may seem perfunctory, but you would be amazed how often this is overlooked in daily practice. The first step is always to ask whether you are looking at a symptom or the root cause.

Your eventual solution will only stick if it addresses the root cause.

To find the root cause:

- **Ask why at least five times.** The problem might be a poorly trained employee – or it could be a process flaw. The problem could be the quality of a raw material – or the capability of a particular machine. Keep digging until you are confident you have found the source – otherwise you will be slapping band-aids on symptoms and the problem will likely recur.

- **Use the team.** Yes, time is short, but problem solving is best described as a team sport. Depending on the nature of the problem to be addressed, one or more of those whom you lead may have deeper insight than you. Do not be rash with problem definition.

- **Seek input from outside the team.** The more important the problem, the greater the need to correctly define the problem. If your team lacks expertise, find it. In addition, the path to solving most problems usually spans multiple groups; thus, seeking input is a form of bridge building that may help you as the process unfolds past problem definition.

Once you have the problem pinned down, 9 times out of 10 you will realize that every outcome is multi-determined. Stated differently, the source of the problem often is not one thing, but several. Ask yourself the following:

- **What are the most important causes?** Always think about the 80/20. Concentrate your efforts on the ones with the biggest likely impact.

- **To what degree are these causes related?** The more related the causes, the more you must focus your efforts on multiple fronts.

- **Who owns each cause?** Socially and politically, what are your chances of actually acting successfully on each cause? The causes can be identified, but is it reasonable to suggest you can address them?

Based on the interdependencies, the politics involved, and your personal power, you will have your short list of causes (targets) that might be worth your time.

Step two is Investigate. Investigating has two major components: to generate possibilities and to evaluate and select the most promising solution(s).

Generating possibilities: This is the most creative part of the problem-solving process – amassing possible paths forward. Individuals and groups find this challenging for many reasons.

- **People cling to the past.** Too often we see current tasks as overly related to past tasks, resulting in less than ideal decisions.

- **Members wish to experience low risk.** Many professionals are apprehensive about being overtly evaluated, thus they censor significantly when creativity is needed.

- **People are not trained on creative problem-solving methods.** Beyond having a mere conversation, there are many useful structured creative idea generating techniques. You cannot use them if you do not know them.

- **Acquiescence to the leader.** Status often unintentionally creates difficult conversations. Thus, people with good ideas regularly censor themselves and accept ideas espoused by the leader of the group.

- **Desire for fast answers.** Many well-intentioned professionals feel a desire to reach conclusions quickly, for personal and professional reasons. Haste often leads to suboptimal decisions.

When you understand the common obstacles above, you can begin to work around them. Key strategies to use in order to facilitate productive problem solving include:

- **Have group members do homework before the meeting.** One of the most difficult times in most decision-making meetings is the very beginning when ideas begin to surface. Make it easy to begin the process by having people arrive with several ideas already generated.

- **Level the playing field.** When selecting attendees for the meeting, err strongly on reducing the number of levels in the hierarchy represented. The lower the status variance, the more robust the conversation.

- **Leaders – do not go / go late.** Your credentials and experience can help a lot – but they can cause damage as well. Once in awhile, have an able lieutenant stand in to create a new group dynamic.

- **Leaders – do not start with your ideas.** Yes, you have good ideas, but do not start with them. Tell the group they exist because you need their expertise and begin with their ideas, or you risk too much acquiescence to your ideas.

- **Follow the classic brainstorming rules.** The first chunk of time is dedicated to generating and capturing ideas and does not allow for idea evaluation. Build on ideas and combine ideas, the wilder the better. The second chunk of time is dedicated to applying agreed upon criteria to reduce the possibilities to an actionable few.

Do not forget, aside from the issue of leaders and status, in a decision-making meeting of this sort, you need input from three particular groups of people:

- **Your normal team members.** The usual bunch who comprise your team, less any specific member who is not intimately involved in the particular decision at hand.

- **Outsiders of interest.** Should you feel/know that the potential solution will involve groups other than your own, representatives might be needed to ensure a quality solution and implementation.

- **Those affected by the outcome.** Think about the main group of employees who will feel the impact of the decision you make. Ideally, they need a voice in your process to increase the odds of successful decision acceptance.

Once a meaningful array of possibilities has been proposed, it is time to evaluate. The time spent thoughtfully evaluating potential solutions should generally increase in proportion to the size of the problem and the time available.

The more important the issue, the more the evaluation process should err towards being rigorous and systematic.

During the evaluation process, be sure to:

- **Use good data**. All data are not created equal. Make sure you understand the assumptions underlying all key facts and figures before using them to make decisions.

- **Use relevant standards**. As the process of narrowing down possibilities unfolds, be explicit as to any and all standards the solution must meet. Any ambiguity here slows you down and often leads to unnecessary conflict.

- **Consider ripple effects**. Every decision you make affects not only the targeted area, but (in varying degrees) other areas as well. That is the nature of the interdependent processes which comprise an organization. When evaluating options, consider all relevant part-whole relationships and the possible effects on nearby parts of the process or business for any given option being considered.

- **Consider unintended outcomes**. All decisions have multiple implications in practice – some intended and some not intended. If you spend a small amount of time thinking about this fact, it is often possible to predict the most likely unintended outcomes, which becomes a factor to consider in choosing a final alternative.

Following the generation and evaluation of alternatives, you make a selection. When you and/or your team make the final selection, be sure your choice:

- **Can actually solve the problem.** Do not satisfice (i.e., do something that is merely "good enough"). No solution is perfect, but for the process to have integrity, the solution needs to be as highly value added as possible given the time and resources available.

- **Is aligned with higher level goals and objectives.** This is a classic – to be useful the solution must not undermine or work counter to other higher-level goals that apply to you and your team.

- **Is financially feasible.** In short, if it breaks the bank, it is not the answer. Find ways to make it more affordable, or try another path.

- **Is politically feasible.** Whether you like it or not, some paths forward will be politically supported and some will not. Depending on the amount of personal status you have – and are willing to expend – decide accordingly.

- **Is owned by someone.** Mutual agreement about a solution without agreement on ownership is one sign of a mediocre group. Who will do what and when must be very specific and publicly agreed upon.

Finally, we Execute the solution. To "execute" means to implement the solution. Start by asking yourself what is needed for successful execution of your chosen solution. Who will be affected and how? Consider how to use each of these:

- **Communication.** Messages about the coming change must be specific, positive, provided with enough lead time to prepare, be clear as to explanations for the change, and must sell the benefits effectively. The larger the portion of the organization affected by the solution, the higher the need to use multiple communication channels and a consistent message.

- **Training.** To effectively adopt the decision you have made, what new skills, if any, will those affected require? Identify them, locate quality training resources, and ensure the training is complete prior to implementation.

- **Resources.** Even if new skill building is not required, are new work tools? This might include software, machines, or actual tools. If you ask employees to do something new, make sure they have the resources to be successful.

- **Structural job changes.** To maximize the impact of your decision, do certain processes or job roles need to be changed – a little or a lot? A solution that does not match the structural capabilities of the current work environment is not an ideal solution.

Next, make a genuine effort to predict the major "bumps in the road" and potential areas of resistance to your solution.

Bumps in the road refer to challenges that crop up after implementation that could not be perfectly predicted beforehand. They tend to be unavoidable, but the major ones can often be anticipated.

Make sure you:

- **Predict both the hard-side and soft-side bumps.** On the hard-side, which process changes, new technologies, or tools have a real likelihood of failing or not operating as intended? On the soft side, which person or group might you reasonably expect to resist the solution?

- **Agree on key contingencies.** When the predictable bumps happen, or when the predictable people resist, what will you do? A cogent answer is required before you begin to implement – otherwise, you risk acting too rashly in the moment.

- **Differentiate bumps from fatal flaws.** Bumps are manageable issues. Fatal flaws stop your solution from working at all. Do not let negative people talk about mere bumps as fatal flaws.

- **Never forget the need to frame positively.** Bumps represent learning opportunities and your team will only view them as such to the extent that you view them as such.

When trying to predict where you might face resistance, consider the following questions:

- **Who will lose power?** If someone perceives they are losing status and power, they might resist.

- **Who will have a changed work load?** If the array of tasks to be completed will be changed, resistance is possible.

- **Who will be asked to use new tools or resources?** Even if the tasks do not change, the means of accomplishing the tasks may change, and thus resistance is possible.

Attempt to deal with your predicted resistors before you actually begin the execution:

- **Consider co-opting.** This means to take a predicted resistor and make them (in some fashion) part of the team making the decision. When they have a voice in the matter it reduces the likelihood they (or others whom they influence) will resist the solution.

- **Sell the benefits.** Whether co-opted or not, ensure the predictable resistors understand the operational and/or strategic importance of adopting the solution.

- **Sell the consequences.** Not adopting might have various consequences including: product/service /process-quality problems, or administrative implications for the resistors. The consequences of non-compliance should be known.

Following the beginning of implementation, when evidence of resistance surfaces:

- **Communicate immediately.** Separate fact from fiction. Investigate quickly, but do not be accusatory. If there is resistance, find the root cause.

- **Intervene with help.** Do not begin with a heavy hand. Begin by seeking to genuinely help. This might involve further explanations or additional resources.

- **Intervene with consequences.** If needed, and if the implementation is important enough, you must do what is required to ensure success. This might involve you (or the appropriate authority) changing someone's role, reprimands, or – in the extreme – removal of someone from their role.

Choose one: Keep the resistor, or make the solution a success.

Finally, effective execution will be facilitated by planning the appropriate timing, pace, feedback, and monitoring.

- **Timing.** Given the nature of your solution, consider calendar-based opportunities and constraints including budget cycles, product launches, holidays, etc. Choose the soonest possible time that allows maximum opportunity for solution success.

- **Pace.** Should you implement in small chunks (i.e., pilot), or all at once? Should you move fast or more conservatively? There are pros and cons to any answer. Your goal is to explore the implications of each prior to executing.

- **Feedback.** Be proactive, not reactive. Have people and mechanisms in place to ensure that once implementation begins, you have quality data upon which to make decisions.

- **Monitoring.** In order to monitor the solution, feedback concerning the actual work tasks being changed must be addressed with specific and appropriate metrics – which must be agreed upon prior to execution.

CHALLENGE:

Review the problem-solving section and identify the elements you and your team neglect most often.

Local Versus Systemic Problems

As you consider the problem-solving process, keep in mind the difference between local problems and systemic problems.

- **Local problems.** Problems largely associated with one individual/group, a simple process, or a discrete part of a larger process. The number of people and the portion of the organization involved are both small.

- **Systemic problems.** Large numbers of people are involved and/or a sizeable amount of the organization is involved.

Your first task is to identify the nature of the problem – local or systemic. Local problems need local solutions and systemic problems need systemic solutions. Unfortunately, many professionals err towards providing systemic solutions for local problems which unnecessarily increases bureaucracy.

For example, if one employee fails to properly adhere to a given process requirement, the person's direct supervisor should address and resolve the matter. It might be the case that this particular person requires an additional tool or resource to correctly complete the job.

Fine – but that does not mean the supervisor should contact other leaders and/or Human Resources and initiate a similar "fix" to this problem that will be applied to everyone else involved in the same type of work.

Every time you fix a local problem with a systemic answer you hurt productivity by wasting a huge number of dollars and hours.

Time and money are limited resources. Only pursue systemic solutions when there is real evidence of systemic problems, not simply the possibility of systemic problems.

FOCUS ON THE RIGHT PROBLEMS

Given the never-ending number of problems addressed each day at work, and our limited time and resources, it is shocking the decisions we make.

The two most common problem-related mistakes we make are allowing too many recurring problems and spending too little time on the most important problems.

Too Many Recurring Problems

When you go to work each week, do you neatly follow your list of things to do? Usually not. Normally, a long list of "fires" pops up unexpectedly screaming to be addressed. Fires happen for many reasons, but one of the best explanations is that the fire is a problem we have seen before yet failed to correctly solve.

We put a temporary fix on it, we apply a short-term "good enough" solution, we put a band-aid on it, and we fail to ensure it will not recur.

How many issues and problems that you face every day have you seen before? A conservative guess would be that 40% to 60% of the problems you face are not new. You faced them last week, last month, or last quarter, but you (and/or your team) failed to devise a plan or solution that just might stop them from coming back around at some point in the future.

Every time we face a problem, we have a choice as to whether we will fix the problem today, or fix the problem for good.

It has been said a million times – for a reason – get to the root cause. Ask "why?" as many times as needed, but either get to the source of the problem and fix it, or pat yourself on the back for having guaranteed that the same problem will come back to haunt you later.

Focus on the Most Important Problems

In line with our discussion of 80/20 thinking, there are two main types of problems: strategic and operational. Both types are important, though the former is far too neglected.

- **Strategic problems.** (aka the 20%) These have more long-term implications. When they are solved, they move your career forward quickly or improve the productivity of your group significantly. They are the ones you need to discover and spend significant time considering.

- **Operational problems.** (aka the 80%) Have more short-term implications. They support the successful continued functioning of the status-quo. They are important, but should consume significantly less time than strategic problems.

For example, operational problems might include improving the customer service process currently in place or improving the product returns policy to improve customer service. In contrast, a strategic problem might be determining how to identify and communicate with a new customer base to ensure a healthy financial future.

Among the array of issues, challenges and problems that you face over time, how many should be of the strategic variety versus the operational variety?

<hr />

CHALLENGE:

If you are a leader, at least half of your time should be spent on strategic problems.

Professionals sometimes fail to allocate their time in this manner because:

- They do not differentiate operational versus strategic problems.

- They do not know how to manage their time effectively.

- The performance management system does not direct their attention properly.

- Their direct supervisor does not direct their attention properly.

A promise:
the speed of your career progress depends much more on your success with strategic problems than with operational problems.

DECISION MAKING

As defined earlier, decision making represents the discrete judgment-call moments that pop up periodically during the problem-solving process. Decisions ensure that you continue moving productively through the process from problem definition to successful execution.

Voting Stinks

It is important to note the most important reason by far for making a particular decision: merit. No other justification ensures the highest likelihood of success, is as honest, or as defensible to others.

Using merit as your one best guide has a few implications.

- **Allow adequate time.** Arriving at a decision based on reason and merit, as free of non-meritorious justifications as possible, takes time. When possible, agree before a meeting begins about how much time is available for deliberations. The more important the problem, the more generous you should be. Finally, manage time productively (see the section on meeting management in the next chapter).

- **Establish ground rules.** Though agreement on the merits is the ideal, it is never the case that everyone can always agree completely. Thus, before beginning decision-making sessions, agree on an acceptable decision-making rule.

Example: The "70% Rule," whereby members agree to be accepting of a decision they do not completely agree with when they are at least 70% in agreement.

- **Avoid Voting.** While there are many decision rules you might use, there is one that tends to be bad all the time: voting. Voting is very expeditious, but in a decision-making context it creates unproductive camps – "us" versus "them." Those who "won" the vote and those who did not. This is efficient, but typically ineffective.

There Are Many Tools

A few common and useful decision-making tools:

- **Pareto analysis**. A simple analysis built on the 80/20 logic resulting in choices that will allow for the biggest impact.

- **Grid or matrix analysis**. This approach allows for a comparison of choices by factors worth considering, producing overall weighted scores for each choice.

- **Paired comparisons**. A matrix approach allowing paired comparisons of all possible choices.

- **Fishbone diagrams**. Diagrams depicting the causes of an event. The diagram typically groups possible causes into these categories: people, methods, machines, materials, measurements, and environment.

- **Force field analysis**. Allows a visual analysis of the forces supporting a particular choice and those opposing the choice.

- **Cost/benefit analysis**. Involves adding up the value of the benefits associated with a choice and subtracting the costs.

- **Decision trees**. Uses a tree-shaped diagram to model the possible decisions and their likely consequences. This approach allows for a series of linked events to be evaluated in terms of both probability and value (cost, revenue, etc.).

- **Risk analysis**. Allows the risk associated with a choice to be assessed by multiplying the probability of an outcome by the cost of the outcome.

There are literally hundreds of additional tools, and software designed to facilitate the use of tools and combinations of tools. When you select a decision-making tool, consider:

- **Cost**. How much will it cost to gather the required data and apply the tool? A particular type of analysis may be known to be useful, but consider the nature of the problem, and ask if it is justified.

- **Time**. Sometimes it may be known precisely which analysis is appropriate at a particular decision point. However, a great rule is to judge the time required conservatively, and err on seeking an expedient decision tool.

- **The need for expertise**. An endless array of decision-making tools exists. Some are very complex and require particular types of expertise. Do not hesitate to seek outside expertise. It might save you from attempting to reinvent the wheel or from facing unnecessary learning curves. This is especially true when time is short.

Head or Gut?

When faced with a problem to solve, it is important to make a conscious choice about the appropriateness of using either the "head" or the "gut."

The head refers to a more systematic approach to problem solving and decision making. The gut refers to quick intuitive decision making. Both can be useful, the trick is to know when to use which approach.

Most books show a greater reverence for systematic approaches as opposed to intuition-driven approaches.

The gut refers to that cumulative pot of great experiences you have pulled together over time. It serves as a somewhat unconscious reference point, or compass that we use when we face a new situation. Your "gut" makes you instinctively lean towards option A instead of B.

There is a lot of evidence that top executives, police, medical doctors, and many other professionals rely on the gut more than anything else. If it is true that time is of the essence, do you really have the luxury of thoughtfully working through a systematic approach to problem solving and decision making? Not always.

Sometimes, relying on the gut subjects you to the

perils of experience. Strangely, there can be a downside to excessive experience. After too much, we sometimes become blind to other opinions and possibilities and we can become too overconfident or arrogant.

The real question is whether the head or the gut is appropriate under particular conditions.

Ask yourself the following two questions:

- **Is the issue before you in the 20%?** If the answer is "yes", err on a more formal thinking process (assuming you have the time).

- **How novel is the current situation?** Most people erroneously see current situations as too similar to things they have seen before. This can lead to applying solutions not well-suited to current circumstances.

If more important, err on the head.
If more novel, err on the head. Otherwise, and when time is short, rely on the gut!

Common Traps to Avoid

This list is far from exhaustive, but it covers the most important areas to consider and will point you in the right direction if further detail is needed. The following are among the most common decision-making traps.

- **Too little/much analysis or research.** Based on perceptions of time or skill deficiencies and strengths, most professionals tend to err on incomplete analysis or excessive analysis. This results in either fast, low-quality decisions, or delayed decisions due to "paralysis by analysis."

- **Failure to clarify assumptions.** Any analysis is only as good as the assumptions underlying the analysis. Make them specific, as realistic as possible, and share them openly for feedback.
- **Being anchored to the past.** Be wary of the extent to which the current situation mimics a past incident. Actively search for what is novel in the present situation.
- **Belief in false constraints.** Most constraints are perceived, not real. People believe something cannot be done, or done in a timely fashion, or that someone will not support them, etc. Differentiate between real and perceived constraints.
- **Poor/insufficient data.** The old saying, "garbage in, garbage out" is correct. A quality analysis requires quality data.
- **Too fast or hasty.** Never sacrifice effectiveness for efficiency if it is not required. The more complex the analysis, the more moderated the pace must be.
- **Failure to predict resistance.** Every decision is not universally loved. However, most major instances of resistance can be predicted before decisions are enacted.
- **Misinterpretation of data.** Based on the pace of analysis or skill level, this is all too common. The best hedge is to slow down and consider getting

another person with the correct expertise involved to examine the more crucial parts of your work.

- **Various cognitive biases.** Normal human beings regularly use faulty thinking for a variety of reasons. There are many common biases. Your best bet is to familiarize yourself with the most damaging ones. The more they are "front of brain" for you, the less likely you will fall prey to them.

DO NOT NEGLECT
THE DEVIL'S ADVOCATE

The devil's advocate is a tremendously important role in any group and for any decision-making context.

The devil's advocate is a person who assumes a contrary position for the sake of argument. This type of action serves as a vital hedge against:

- **Decisions supported by weak logic**. In the heat of discussion, when people are tired, or when information is imperfect, poor logic may seem momentarily sensible. The devil's advocate attempts to shine a light on this possibility.

- **Hasty decisions**. We sometimes hurry and neglect deliberate thinking. The devil's advocate helps groups slow down and consider their thought processes more carefully.

- **Decisions not based on merit**. When decisions are based wholly or partially on politics, past precedent, or other interesting but not ideal standards, the devil's advocate is the person who speaks up and questions the group.

It is equally important to be clear about what the devil's advocate is not:

- **A "squeaky wheel."** This is a person who tends to be a loud complainer and is often doing so as a means of securing or protecting resources. Some squeaky wheels do not need to be oiled – they need to be replaced!

- **A fault finder**. This is the person capable of suggesting plausible logical faults, but who is unwilling or unable to offer constructive and productive comments about moving forward.

- **An obstructionist**. A person uncomfortable with change who tends to react negatively to all proposed decisions.

The devil's advocate, in many groups is not supported positively. People choose not to support, or to negatively engage the devil's advocate because:

- **They feel the person is "causing trouble."** When people hear opposing or critical views, they too often prematurely assume the person is being hostile instead of helpful.

- **They are adding time to the process.** Sometimes others assume the benefit provided by the devil's advocate will be small or nonexistent, thus they resent extra time being added to the process.

- **They do not like being questioned.** With rare exceptions, people do not enjoy being questioned. Thus, when the devil's advocate assumes a position that is in opposition to theirs, they become irritated.

Great leaders find a way to validate the devil's advocate, even when they do not initially like the perceived opposition they represent.

Validate the devil's advocate by:

- **Genuinely asking for it**. Given the risks inherent in being the devil's advocate, it is the responsibility of the leader to reinforce the importance of this role.

- **Defending the validity of the role**. When the devil's advocate speaks, do not treat them adversely. One particularly harsh reaction to an honest devil's advocate and the role may cease to exist in the group.

- **Occasionally play the role yourself.** As a leader, there is no better way to establish a norm than to model the behavior yourself. Your actions will speak louder than your words.

Normally, one or two members of a team will be naturally inclined to assume the role of the devil's advocate. However, this role will have the greatest impact when it becomes a shared role. Consider having the role filled by a different member of the team each week until the team gains comfort with the presence of the devil's advocate.

CHALLENGE:
Reflect on how often you:
1) support/do not support the Devil's Advocate,
and 2) play the role when needed.

Here is one last thought on problem solving and decision making:

Your decisions will not make everyone happy all the time.

Your goal is not to make everyone happy.

To the best of your ability, your goal is to make decisions that will maximize the long-term value of the organization.

6

CONFLICT IS NOT A DIRTY WORD

CONFLICT GETS A BAD WRAP

Conflict is underrated. It is often defined as bad, but that is overly simplistic. To begin, you must separate positive conflict from negative conflict.

Your job as a leader is to stop creating or allowing negative conflict while figuring out how to create and validate positive conflict.

To be specific:

- **Negative conflict**. Tends to be unplanned, usually involves personality clashes, overindulges in emotions and opinions, does not follow rules, and lacks facilitation by others resulting in lower productivity and strained relationships.

- **Positive conflict**. Tends to be planned, typically involves the discussion of relevant work-related issues, focuses on facts/emotions are tempered, follows agreed upon rules, and is productively facilitated by others resulting in higher productivity while maintaining or improving relationships.

Let us briefly consider the major facets of these definitions:

- **How conflict begins**. It begins either randomly when one or more individuals "lose it" and engage in unproductive interactions, or in a planned thoughtful manner. Random conflict is usually unproductive.

Planned conflict is not guaranteed to succeed, but the odds of success are far greater versus random conflict.

- **The object of conflict**. Can be unproductive or productive. Typically, unproductive conflict does not involve interesting work-related issues. It involves trivial work issues or personality and attitude-related issues. Productive conflict usually involves important work-related issues which, if addressed properly, have the potential to move the group forward.

- **Issues and emotions**. Your goal is always to deal in facts. Nonetheless, data are not always available, or of high quality, leading to the inevitable use of opinions. Caution, the more people deal in opinions, the more people can become emotional and lean on unsubstantiated positions.

- **Referees and rulebooks**. For conflict to be productive, it cannot be a spectator sport. Norms (rules) must exist, the team (referees) must be involved in the dialogue, and the leader (also a referee) must steer the dialogue as productively as possible ensuring adherence to the norms.

- **The results of conflict**. Can be good or bad depending on the severity of the conflict and the presence of quality conflict management skills. Generally, if the participants have quality conflict management skills, better decisions and higher productivity result.

The Rules of Positive Conflict

To create and keep positive conflict, follow a few rules:

- Address the issue, not the person.

- Address behaviors, not perceived intentions.

- State what you want and why.

- Use positive language, frame statements positively.

- Do not interrupt while others are speaking.

- Show emotions, but keep the extremes in check.

- Stick to the facts, be wary of opinions.

- Avoid the BLAME game.

- If you criticize, be open to criticism.

- Stay on track, do not bring up largely unrelated issues.

None of these represent magic bullets, but if they become mutually agreed upon and adhered to group norms, they will effectively manage both planned and unplanned conflict.

Mediating Conflict

When conflict does erupt (whether positive or negative), here are a few good mediation tips to consider that will steer you and your team in a productive direction.

For those who are not directly involved in the conflict, the major goals include:

- **Begin by listening**. If you want the team to develop good positive conflict skills, you have to let the conversation begin without you immediately micro-managing and trying to mediate for a fast resolution.

- **Call it conflict**. When tensions rise too much, it is very useful to state that you can feel it, i.e., that conflict is rising – in the moment. When that label is used, participants tend to become more thoughtful about how to proceed.

- **Ensure adherence to the rules**. The rules work only when you follow them. When the team sees a violation, they have to call it. Otherwise, they are merely contributing to the conflict.

- **Add input when needed**. If anyone has data or information that bears on the conversation at hand, offer it. Also, facts are often interpreted differently by different professionals. Thus it is not only new data that might be added, but new perspectives.

- **Spot common ground**. Many times there is shared agreement between two or more people engaged in a conflict situation, yet they do not see it. The referees can more easily identify the common ground and point it out.

- **Resist taking sides**. Your integrity will be enhanced when you are perceived as following the facts. Think broadly and consider the implications for the team instead of, "playing favorites."

- **Try to keep it balanced**. Based on personality or other factors, the conversation can become lopsided. You want to facilitate a dialogue, not a one-way tirade.

- **Stop and reschedule**. If you are the leader and sense extreme emotions or complete lack of progress after a few minutes, consider stopping the conversation. Follow up with the main participants individually in private before beginning public conversation again.

CHALLENGE:
How often are you and your colleagues filling these roles when you experience conflict at work?

AVOID CONFLICT AT YOUR OWN RISK

Why should you care about engaging the difficult process of conflict management? Quite simply, you must manage it, otherwise it will manage you.

An inability to effectively deal with conflict can derail your career.

In terms of dealing with conflict, there are generally three types of people.

- **The passives (70% of people)**. They habitually avoid conflict. Negative conflict that is avoided almost always resurfaces later – and it usually grows. When you avoid conflict, you tell others about your will and character. When positive conflict is avoided, improvement potential is lost – possibly forever.

- **The potentials (20% of people)**. They understand the potential of positive conflict. However, they fail to adequately check the emotions and they do not possess strong conflict-management skills. Best of intentions aside, they make things worse.

- **The professionals (10% of people)**. They understand the potential of positive conflict and they have at least decent emotional intelligence and strong conflict management skills. This is the small group of people whom you should aspire to join.

CHALLENGE:
Successful leadership teams are 10/20/70, not 70/20/10. What is your team?

Your career success depends on your joining the "professionals" group. Leaders are hired and promoted based on their ability to successfully engage in various types of growth through creativity and innovation. Inevitably, this involves dealing effectively with conflict.

If you believe in the 80/20 rule and the power of positive conflict, you have to consider the possibility of sometimes dealing with people whom you would rather avoid. If you cannot view the following in a positive light, you will not enjoy leadership roles:

- **You will always work with people whom you do not like**. Unless you work in complete solitude, this is a simple fact of life. How you view it is up to you.

- **They know and do things you need**. Not only do you not like them, but they have skills you need in order to be successful. Thus, your career growth requires them.

- **You must find a way to productively co-exist**. In fact, you must move past mere tolerance towards genuine appreciation. How you feel about a professional colleague cannot be "all or nothing."

NO JERKS ALLOWED

Opportunities for positive conflict abound: we need to discuss an unproductive team dynamic that we have allowed to fester, we need to address how to improve one of our key processes, it is vital we find and talk about the root cause of that quality issue, and so on.

Leaders must identify opportunities for positive conflict, speak up and facilitate the dialogue, validate the input offered by others, and celebrate the progress positive conflict can bring.

However, while supporting participation in positive conflict, the leader cannot support jerks.

Jerks are: rude, demean others, negatively personalize issues, pick on people, take too much credit, and in general are not liked by most of the team.

Actually, there are two types of jerks at work:

- **The everyday jerk**. The vast majority of jerks fall into this category. Believe it or not, most jerks are meaningfully unaware they are perceived as jerks by their colleagues. They are not malicious. They are simply clueless and a pain to work with.

- **The evil people**. Some jerks are aware of their status and do not care. That is evil, pure and simple.

Some jerks are highly skilled employees. On the task side, they add a lot of value. As a result, many jerks are regularly tolerated due to their superior performance.

No amount of amazing performance justifies consistent jerk-like behaviors.

If you do not deal with them:

- **They get worse**. A jerk who does not experience negative consequences due to their behaviors is a jerk whose bad tendencies will increase.

- **They multiply**. Jerkiness is contagious! One jerk at work unchecked can become multiple jerks quickly.

- **They hurt morale and productivity**. Left unchecked, morale is predictably going to drop, and productivity typically follows suit.

- **They damage your reputation**. If you are the boss, expect others to lose respect for you. No matter how good the jerk is at the job, if you allow them to be a jerk, folks might start to think you are a jerk too.

If you feel you have a jerk on your hands, follow these steps:

- **Decide: is this an isolated incident or a pattern**? Do not intervene for a mild isolated incident. If you see more than three mild (or worse) incidents in a fairly short span of time, the rule is: three strikes and they are a jerk.

- **Decide: is this merely irksome or a hit to productivity or morale**? If the jerk is an irritant, but not really causing harm, err on not intervening. Otherwise, proceed to the next point.

- **Provide private feedback**. State your view of their jerk status (follow the rules of effective communication), be particularly careful to be specific and check your emotions.

- **Provide a private reprimand**. If feedback does not work, formalize by using a letter in their file and/or comments on an evaluation. You must also set new, clear, behavioral expectations.

- **Change their role**. For all but the truly evil jerks, the above will suffice. If needed, rescope their role to mitigate the damage they can cause.

- **Remove them from the company**. This is a difficult last resort that is sometimes far wiser than attempting to develop the person any further.

Start a discussion on your team about what your norms are relative to the jerk issue.

DEALING WITH A STICKY SITUATION

Here is a quick take on a famous and quite useful model for managing conflict[1].

Each option differently balances the need to assert your position with the possibility of giving others what they want. Whether dealing with negative or positive conflict, these are your major choices:

- **Avoiding**. This is typically not productive. It tends to make conflict worse. The one caveat involves the 80/20 rule. Strategically, you cannot fight for every issue, thus avoiding can have some utility in the long-run.

- **Accommodating**. Refers to giving someone what they want regardless of what you want. Done too much, it can turn you into a doormat. However, as with avoiding, it can be useful as a long-term strategic option.

- **Compromising**. This is the old give and take, "quid pro quo," I get something and you get something. It is a decent option many times. The problem is that no

---

[1] Ruble, T. L., & Thomas, K. W. (1976). Support for a two-dimensional model of conflict behavior. Organizational Behavior and Human Performance, 16, 143-155.

party gets all they want. Further, if you compromise too quickly, people come to expect it.

- **Collaborating**. This represents the idealized "win/win" where, through ingenuity and hard work, we both get all we need. This is difficult and rare since it requires lots of extra time, genuine empathy, and creative problem solving.

- **Forcing**. This is the "my-way-or-the-highway" approach, which almost always leaves a bad taste in people's mouths and should not be your first thought. However, in a crisis or to ensure safety, it can be justified – and will be viewed as legit if you provide a great explanation and if you participate with the team in whatever endeavor you are forcing.

When you find yourself at a point in a conversation, or in a project where there is unease and growing disagreement about an issue, you must actively think about which of the above paths will be most advantageous for you.

From a broader perspective, engaging conflict intentionally is part and parcel to change and improvement. It is, however, not a risk free proposition. To be successful, be sure to choose your battles wisely, understand your social capital, and do the homework.

Step 1 – Choose Your Battles Wisely

Engaging a conflict is not something you do without planning. As mentioned earlier, this is all about the 80/20. You cannot and should not engage every issue you want to engage. The issue had better be important if you are going to put the following at risk:

- **Time**. It takes time to properly prepare and time to engage the issue across different contexts (e.g., meetings, personal conversations, research and analysis).

- **Reputation**. Your reputation is a prized asset. Like trust, it is difficult to build over time, yet easy to bruise. Conflict represents a possible threat to your reputation depending on how you handle the process and whether or not you "win."

- **Relationships**. Conflict does not exist in a vacuum. You engage it in opposition to people – people you often need to continue working with productively after moving past the current conflict. Take care not to unduly damage key relationships.

- **Work load**. Related to the issue of time, it is often the case that to the extent you are successful in a conflict management situation, you will have created new work for yourself and/or others. Know this before engaging the issue.

The issue might be in your 20% if most of the following are true:

- **Valuable outcomes are expected**. The issue represents a genuine opportunity to significantly improve the team and or the team's productivity.

- **There is a competitive imperative**. Customers expect

it and the competition does it. To not do this could lead to losing customers and revenue, or strategic partners.

- **Other factors require this change.** Not changing hampers other processes. For example, if we do not change this process, policy, or practice we will not be able to attract and hire the type of professionals we desire.

- **There is a moral or ethical imperative.** The issue must be addressed because it is "the right thing to do" or is needed from a legal perspective.

- **Mission/vision centrality.** To engage this issue is part and parcel to supporting the organization's mission and vision.

- **Personal strategic utility.** Engaging the issue will build bridges between you and other individuals or groups whom you wish to be associated with in the long-term. In short, it is a good career move.

Step 2: Understand Your Social Capital

One important consideration when thinking through a possible conflict situation is the amount of social capital you possess and wish to spend.

Social capital is an intangible asset amassed over time. It represents the amount of personal latitude and freedom you have at work to advance your views, speak up, engage conflict, and generally not adhere to norms.

You can think of social capital as chips one might spend, as in the game of poker. The chips you build up or earn over time are a function of several things:

- **Tenure**. Mere tenure should not justify the acquisition of chips (as would strong performance), though it often does.

- **Track record**. A more intellectually satisfying explanation as opposed to tenure, and more potent. Nothing earns more chips than amazing performance.

- **Charisma & likeability**. This is not about performance, but about how people generally feel about you as a person and as a colleague. Whether fair or not, this can be a powerful source of social capital.

- **Helpfulness**. Similar to charisma, this is not about your performance, but about how you relate to others. People love genuinely helpful colleagues and friends.

- **Who you know**. You are part of a network. The strength of your network has a strong impact on how others view your ideas and suggestions.

Ask yourself how much social capital you have in the bank. Is your account low, adequate, or full? This is admittedly difficult to judge since some people are very skilled at judging these types of personal issues while others are not. Nonetheless, you need to consider this issue.

You can get a rough estimate on the size of your social capital account by considering the following:

- **Your recent performance history**. Consider both your most recent performance evaluation as well as informal feedback you may have received. The better your job performance, the more chips you have.

- **Your recent interpersonal exchanges**. Regarding the people whose support you might seek: have you had positive relations, negative relations, mixed relations? The more positive, the more chips you have.

- **Your formal status relative to a target issue**. The size of your account does vary a bit depending on the issue and how related your title and expertise are to the issue at hand. The more closely they are tied, the more chips you have.

- **Others' opinions of you**. Others always perceive you differently than you do. Find a few confidants who will be honest and ask them about how much social capital you have.

Step 3 – Do the Homework

In the first step you decided to engage the issue. In the second step you determine you are willing and able to spend some of your social capital. The third step requires you to complete several key activities before you actually start espousing your view on the issue.

- **Do you have a snowball's chance?** Think about the leaders above you in the organization. Based on what you know about them, their experience, their loyalties, and their recent decisions – would you expect them to support your position?

- **Paint a picture**. Can you vividly describe the interesting and valuable end state to be achieved should they decide to accept your position? Be able to quickly describe why it is so worth achieving (to the group, customers, etc.).

- **Stick to the facts**. Do not rely on opinions, innuendo, half-truths, unproven bold assertions or your "perspective" on the matter. Start with and faithfully stick to the facts.

- **Bring your friends**. You want a decent grip on your odds. Do the leg work and find out where everyone stands. The more friends you have (those who share your view on the issue), the better your odds.

- **Turn lemons into lemonade**. Be able to articulate how your position actually helps the opposition. It is difficult for them to disagree with you when your solution in some way helps them.

- **Make it a no-brainer for the leadership team**. If you were given the green light today from your boss, how would you sell this idea to senior leaders? Be able to articulate in a few short and ultra coherent bullets how your position supports the company's higher-level goals and objectives.

- **Admit your culpability!** Do not BLAME others. Fess up to your role in the status quo instead. When you admit your role in the calamity, the opposition is more likely to be positively engaged in the discussion.

- **Validate points with which you agree**. Try to find some part of the opposition's position with which you can agree. Your goal is to build some honest mutual respect that will help them want to listen to your position.

- **Offer solutions, not problems**. If you are going to raise difficult issues, you need good ideas. Have something articulate to say about how we might change the status quo on this issue or seriously consider biting your tongue.

- **Finally, get ready to volunteer!** If you are going to ask others to help you make change, you had better be the first one standing in line ready to donate your precious time for the cause.

A Note on Diversity

The common mantra is diversity = good. However, that is not terribly accurate or useful. The truth is diversity usually hurts before it helps.

Diversity has the potential to broaden perspectives and enhance our creative decision-making capacity. However, that potential is not realized as often as should be the case.

The workforce is increasingly diverse in terms of race, gender, and age. There are many bases of diversity. However, in the end, these categories of differences are not useful.

What is useful is how they contribute to the diversity of thought.

To harness the power of diversity, understand that:

- **Diversity makes people uncomfortable**. An age old self-protective tendency is for people to react less than positively to those who look, think, and act differently than they do. This tendency is understandable and predictable, but not productive.

- **Diversity can help if leaders model the way**. When leaders move past the rhetoric and thoughtfully act in a manner supportive of diversity, others begin to follow suit.

- **Diversity can help if the team has decent conflict skills**. When you follow the conflict management rules and guidelines noted earlier, diversity moves past a focus on differences and towards being a catalyst for improved performance.

- **No amount of diversity training trumps thoughtful conversations within a group**. Training might build sensitivity, though it often hurts as much as it helps. Real change related to embracing diversity begins with words and actions within the group on the job.

To be clear, diversity is an amazing asset and an increasingly unavoidable reality. Build your conflict management skills and soon enough you will see how diversity can enrich your team.

THE IMPORTANCE OF FORGIVENESS

No discussion of conflict is complete without mentioning the healing wonder of forgiveness. Here is a great rule of thumb:

If you do not find yourself in need of forgiveness or needing to offer an apology once in a while, you are not being aggressive enough in your pursuit of positive conflict.

When you forgive someone you voluntarily let go of resentment and anger you feel towards a person and/or an issue. You have granted the person the gift of a clean slate and you have granted yourself the gift of not having to shoulder unneeded negativity and spite.

If you are an upwardly mobile leader, you must be forgiving because:

- **You will need forgiveness at some point**. Your odds of being forgiven for mild professional transgressions increases in direct proportion to how well you are able to forgive others.

- **It is the right thing to do**. This book rarely tries to dictate morality, but most agree, there is little justification for holding a grudge. Eventually, the correct course of action is to forgive.

- **It is a key ingredient for group health**. Forgiving is not simply about you and an adversary. It is about making a contribution to the overall health of the group of which you are but one part.

Consider asking for forgiveness when:

- **You sense or know you have upset someone**. We vary in terms of our ability to sense when we have upset others. Try asking someone if you have upset them. Even if they are not completely honest, pay attention to their word choice and non-verbal cues and you may learn a lot.

- **You broke a norm or rule, intentionally or not**. If you become aware that you have broken a formal or informal standard, it might be time to apologize. However, never forget, it is often easier to ask for forgiveness than permission!

- **The relationship in question is strategically important**. Back to the 80/20 – when in doubt, if the person or group is of long-term importance, err on the side of seeking forgiveness.

- **You are losing productivity thinking about the issue**. If you find yourself preoccupied, thinking about whether or not you are somehow guilty – stop wasting time, go talk to the person, and consider asking for forgiveness.

If you honestly want to be forgiven, be prepared to:

- **Check the emotions**. Address the issue after both you and the other party has had time to allow emotions to dissipate.

- **Get feedback**. To obtain a more well rounded view of the situation you have created, seek the perspective of at least one other well informed observer prior to seeking forgiveness from your target.

- **Find the right time**. For less severe issues, public comments during normal meetings or interactions are fine. When wounds are deep, it is best to seek forgiveness privately as a first step.

- **Own what you did**. Do not say, "I acted inappropriately." Be concrete and address specific behaviors.

- **Acknowledge their pain**. Healing begins when you can honestly state that you are aware you offended or hurt them in some fashion.

- **Offer an apology**. After stating the facts and acknowledging the outcome, provide an authentic "I'm sorry."

- **State what you have learned**. As a result of this episode, share what you have learned that will help you avoid such an unproductive faux pas in the future.

- **Listen to their feedback**. Be sure to allow time for them to offer whatever feedback they feel is necessary. Do not interrupt – allow them to clear the air if needed.

- **Make amends**. Be ready to make a specific statement about how you will "make things right" given what you have done. This might include expectation setting regarding your future behavior on this issue.

Finally, these efforts must be sincere. If you accurately follow the prescription above and yet your subsequent behaviors do not follow accordingly, your words will be seen as rhetoric.

CHALLENGE:

Think back over the last twelve months about every conflict with which you have been involved. Can you identify at least one person whom might deserve an apology?

7

THE TRUTH ABOUT GROUPS & TEAMS

There has been a ridiculous amount of writing aimed at explaining the difference between "groups" and "teams." Many writers like to differentiate groups and teams by suggesting that a group of people is nothing special, but a team has a shared goal, a mission, a purpose, etc. This is silly wordplay. I will use the terms interchangeably, because:

Groups and teams are the same thing!

The rise of groups and teams as the preferred structure for accomplishing work in organizations has been building for decades. They have always been around, but now the team is seen as the Holy Grail. Pundits, gurus, and scholars have taken it to another level.

The truth is that teams can be wonderful, but are generally overrated.

GROUPS CAN BE A PAIN

Groups can be useful, but only if they are staffed and facilitated properly. Otherwise, they can be a pain in the butt.

The first thing you need to know about groups is to forget about them and realize the power of competent individuals. Behind most great ideas, there is an individual or two who were the catalysts, the ones who provided the spark. They build teams, and these teams later build organizations.

How successful would these teams have been without these fascinating individuals?

Groups are mini bureaucracies. They come with a lot of overhead that can be horribly unproductive. Consider:

- **Meetings.** Meetings are habitually less productive than they should be, take more time than is needed, and people do not like them.

- **Time for coordinating internally.** When not in meetings, there is still a lot of time spent on members sharing ideas, seeking affirmation or permission, synching documents or databases, etc.

- **Time for coordinating externally**. Other teams and members of the leadership team sometimes need to be consulted and brought up to speed. Sometimes the bigger a group is, the more others expect to formally hear from them.

- **Conflict**. Where there is more than one person, there is the potential for conflict. Though conflict can be productive, it is often the case that our ability to staff and manage our work loads and moods is not perfect, making negative conflict common in group settings.

- **Shirking**. This refers to the tendency we have to contribute less as group size increases. If the group is small, people step up – there is no hiding. The larger you get, the less any one individual feels their contribution is vital, thus they become occasional "wall flowers."

Err Towards Small Team Size

What is the ideal team size? The best answer is the smallest number of people required to get the job done (on time, on budget, with the right quality). When in doubt, do not put the person on the team.

A rule to live by:
always err on fewer people for the team.

The reason is simple, but profoundly important. It is relatively easy to add people to a group. Removing a person from a group is a hugely difficult task by comparison. It might convey to the person:

- They are not liked.
- They are not skilled.
- They are not appreciated.

In addition, the person doing the removing may fear several possible nasty outcomes, such as:

- They will speak poorly of me (and the group).
- They will not cooperate with me (and the group) as needed in the future.
- They will obstruct my work in the future (via committees, interpersonal relationships, etc.).

Thus, not only do we have a tendency to make the group initially too large, but we fear conflict so much that we avoid removing redundant or unneeded people.

When trying to embrace the need to err on fewer people consider a model that relies on a core team and a peripheral team.

The following is true for nearly any task or project: the skills needed at the beginning of the project or task differ from the skills needed in the middle which differ from the skills needed near the end.

Logically, this means the mix of people in a group should vary over time.

If not, you risk having people on the team who are not contributing at certain points in time. Thus, the core team and the peripheral team:

- **The core team.** Even though the skills of any one individual are needed in different amounts over time, it is vital to have continuity in leadership to chart progress, collect institutional knowledge, and provide ownership. A small number of core members must stay for the duration.

- **The peripheral team.** These are specialists brought in for discrete functions (for example, advising on a technical issue). They are wonderful contributors who are nonetheless needed only for short periods of time.

The core team will be the keepers of all things learned as the work unfolds. They are in charge of project management duties. They are the focus of accountability.

Given their huge responsibility, you must work diligently to build a strong core team. You have two major staffing goals: covering the most vital skill areas needed and allowing chemistry to trump skill.

Begin by thinking in terms of the 80/20 – what is the array of hard and soft skills that will be essential for the project's success? The core team needs to address most or all of the 20%. The peripheral team tackles the 80% as needed.

Assuming you have the 20% covered, the chemistry has to be evident. Chemistry refers to the quality of the collective soft-side skills possessed by the team. Good chemistry is indicated by:

- Rapid, open, and honest performance conversations
- Little or no negative conflict
- Modest amounts of positive conflict
- Faster performance correction
- Little to no individual grandstanding
- Strong morale and camaraderie
- Abundant collaboration and helpfulness

Chemistry can be difficult to judge initially and often takes time to develop. However, you improve your odds of achieving it by:

- Defining positive group norms (discussed below)

- Staffing only one or two "chiefs," but not more (i.e., people with a strong desire to lead)

- Excluding any employee known to possess a challenging personality

- Modeling the way (be very aware of your example)

- Including social time for the group (non-work interactions often build work-based chemistry)

The value of amazing skills possessed by one or more individuals is easily lost when the group has no chemistry.

Staff Based on Merit

The single best reason for putting someone on your team is merit: they provide something of real value you need in terms of the task at hand (a mix of needed hard and soft skills). Arguably, this is the only valid reason.

Unfortunately, there are other common (though unwise) criteria used to select team members:

- **Prior association with these types of issues.** Either on past projects or as a regular part of their role, they have relevant expertise. This does not mean they are a fit for the current project. Maybe this person should be on the peripheral team, or a non-participant. If needed, manage expectations by explaining your decision to the non-selected, but do not choose them simply to avoid the conversation.

- **Political Connections**. Often we believe it will be wise to select members who are favored by powerful others or who are connected to powerful others. There are instances where this has merit, but usually it does not and causes more problems than it solves.

- **Friendships**. Friendships at work are not bad, though they can be unproductive at times. One instance is when others perceive (right or wrong) that a staffing decision was unduly influenced by personal friendship. Avoid overindulging in your friends and stay focused on targeting the skills needed.

To give any team the very best chance for success, the members need to start off believing in the integrity of team member selection!

Establish Group Norms

Organizations are full of rules, regulations, and policies – formal standards that govern many of the things we do. Usually, violating these standards is associated with negative outcomes.

In contrast, norms are informal, unwritten standards. Sometimes they are created by default without much thought. To ensure they develop and evolve productively, they should be discussed, agreed upon, and enforced intentionally.

**Informal norms have more power
to shape behavior than formal rules,
regulations, and policies.**

There is no perfect list of group norms since every group is different. The first time the team sits down to kick-off a project, norms should be one of the first items discussed. They might include things you value, things you agree to do, or things you agree not to do.

- **Things you value**. For example: respect for group members, a strong work ethic, or group loyalty.

- **Things you agree to do**. For example: doing what you say you will do, being on time, or being prepared.

- **Things you agree not to do**. For example: be late to meetings, ridicule the opinions of others, or make rash decisions.

A norm can positively shape behavior if and only if it is:

- **Overtly specified**. Don't leave norms to evolve by happenstance, be intentional.

- **Mutually agreed upon**. A norm cannot work unless 100% of the team genuinely agrees.

- **Referred to often**. The single best way to ensure the team stays aware of norms is to post them where the team normally meets – use visual reminders.

- **Enforced when violated**. A potentially powerful norm is useless unless there are actual consequences when it is violated.

If you have an established group and are considering the best way to facilitate their work, assume that meetings are not the ideal way to accomplish your work. Instead, rely on:

- **More individual work**. The more specific tasks and groups of tasks that can be assigned to and owned by one person, the more likely the work moves forward quickly.

- **More subgroup work**. The more tasks or groups of tasks that can be addressed by small subgroups of your members, the more likely the work moves forward quickly.

- **More electronic collaborative tools**. There is a long list of collaborative tools from email to video conferencing to groupware to brainstorming software. They allow work to move forward without incurring as much of the overhead normally associated with traditional meetings.

All of these are hedges against too many unproductive face-to-face meetings.

You can still build quality morale and esprit de corps without excessive face-to-face meeting time!

KEY TEAM ROLES

No matter what type of team you are leading, there are certain generic roles worth mentioning. All of them can easily be described as one of three types: task, social, or negative.

Task roles concern aspects of the tasks and key processes. Social roles concern all of the people-related issues, the "soft" roles that facilitate social cohesion. The negative roles represent habitually unproductive behaviors that must be stamped out.

Any person can hold any role at any time, but most people tend to naturally fill the same roles over time given their personality.

Anyone who regularly fills multiple task and social roles is a superstar. Appreciate them!

If anyone regularly fills multiple negative roles, be ashamed of your hiring process and/or the fact that you and the group are avoiding a confrontation that needs to happen.

Task Roles

Task roles include the roles that help us actually get the work done successfully. "The Expert" is not listed below as one of the key roles because if the group was staffed correctly, everyone will be a relevant expert.

Here are the major task roles to consider: the Director,

Mr. Data, the Task Master, Dr. Process, the Practical One, and the Dreamer.

The problem you are trying to avoid is having too many of one role and not enough of another. Most high performing teams have a balance of these:

- **Director**. Whether formally in charge, or informally due to charisma or expertise, they direct the show. They have the ability to secure resources, give good advice, and are loud voices in proposing goals, tasks, and responsibilities.

- **Mr. Data**. This person is ultra-sensitive to the need for information and numbers. They do not want innuendo, opinions, hunches, or guesses – just the facts. They hate ambiguity. They know when the group needs particular information and they find it. Be wary of timelines – the less time left, the more you have to manage Mr. Data because at some point you have to make decisions and move on.

- **The Task Master**. This person is particularly sensitive to time and responsibilities. They are always reminding people how much time they have left to work on a task or project. Sometimes they can be averse to the social aspects of the group, since they do not like to "waste time." They might rub you the wrong way, but they are important and will keep the group on track.

- **Dr. Process**. This person's obsession is correct adherence to process. They actively look for violations or deviations from sound practices. They will attend to interdependencies and proper sequence. For example, Dr. Process will call someone out if they are trying to solve a problem before it has been properly defined. They are also good at spotting violations of group norms.

- **Practical One**. This person is level-headed, even-keeled, sensible, full of common sense, in touch with reality and aware of constraints. They provide a constant validity check as work unfolds. They also see how the group's work might ruffle some feathers in other areas of the firm or with some external party, and raise the caution flag. So long as the Practical One is not too loud or too quick to speak up, they keep you safe.

- **Dreamer**. Sometimes, you need to play it safe and stick to the rules. Other times, you need to get a little wacky or radical. Say hello to the Dreamer. They see possibilities and connections and they love the word "why." Ambiguity and the unknown do not frighten them. The main trick is to encourage them more when generating possibilities and contain them a little more when it is time to make and execute decisions.

Social Roles

This set of behaviors is not about doing the work per se, but refers instead to dealing correctly with people while doing the work.

If you do not have these roles nailed, no amount of task skill will be effective.

There are four key social roles in groups: The Spark, the Peace Maker, the Comedian, and the Helper. Again, people typically play multiple roles, so keep your eyes peeled for a nice balance of these:

- **Spark**. This is possibly the most crucial role. They provide the biggest infusion of energy, provide excitement, a positive perspective, and lots of encouragement. They exude positive emotion and have no problem seeing the glass half full.

- **Peacemaker**. It is true, on occasion we need to ignore them and pursue positive conflict. However, when you are dealing with smaller conflicts, silly or petty personality clashes, or even huge conflicts that threaten to destroy the very fabric of the group, the Peacemaker can be a lifesaver. They validate others, point out common ground, and in general are good at diffusing the level of tension in a situation.

- **Comedian**. Another way to diffuse conflict is by using humor. Sometimes the Peacemaker can do this, but it is best left to a Comedian. They tell a funny joke or story, make a funny face, remind the group about a funny memory, or somehow get others to laugh at the absurdity of the conflict. In the process, they build perspective and soothe nerves. However, be cautious. Comedy and humor are best left to the Comedians and should not be forced. One less than thoughtful joke can really escalate a conflict.

- **Helper**. They are the best type of do-gooder. They want the group to be successful and want each individual to be successful. They like it when things work so they try to make it happen by looking for ways to help. This desire to make the team successful often makes the Helper the team's best utility player. They tend not to complain, put in tons of effort, and are typically liked by everyone.

CHALLENGE:
Which one or more of these roles define you? Should others as well?

Negative Roles

You must face up to reality and admit that sometimes people can be downright problematic. All is not lost because, just as we know that conflict happens, so does the occasional negative group member.

Luckily, most negative group members can be managed. The worst among them are: the Dominator, the Paralyzer, the Gut, the Wall Flower, and the dreaded Prima Donna.

- **Dominator**. This refers to the obstinate talking head in your group who just cannot keep their mouth shut. They always have something to say – and can be belligerent about it. They are too quick to argue, interrupt, raise their voice, and start unnecessary conflict. In a meeting, they are the worst – locked in a room with plenty of victims to terrorize. Manage the Dominator by:

- Briefly acknowledge and validate their view, but then give the focus of the conversation to another group member. In essence, you are taking away their microphone.

- If they start to unproductively dominate again, take the focus again and give it to yourself. They are less likely to trample you, the leader.

- Against the odds, if they continue, directly address them by pointing out the need to hear the rest of the group.

- In rare cases, even the direct approach fails. That is when it is time to speak to the person off-line and deliver excellent feedback and new expectations.

- **Paralyzer**. They exemplify the saying "paralysis by analysis." They hate ambiguity, and cannot resist any attempt to say "what if." They want more time than is humanly possible to consider the situation, plan, analyze, plot and graph, check, recheck, and then check some more. They love spreadsheets. They have never ever finished a task early, because that would be time wasted not redoing work which has already been completed. You manage the Paralyzer as follows:

  - Start by telling them thanks for such genuine attention to the details.

- Reference the deadlines which are looming.

- Remind them of relevant group norms, especially those concerning decision making.

- Redirect them by specifically assigning a new deliverable.

• **Gut**. They do not really enjoy data. They are very intuitive and feel the right course of action is knowable based on hunches and past experience. They want to be uber efficient so badly that they are willing to move forward before having all the facts. They are annoyed at the thoughtful types who wish to effectively use all available time to make decisions. To manage the Guts:

- Communicate the importance of making a quality decision.

- Stress the need for due diligence to the extent there is time to do so – ask them for data to back up their position.

- Task them with exploring one of the other major ideas being considered to provide a more useful comparison.

• **Wall Flowers**. They might be quiet, but could still be a problem since they do not put in their fair share of work. I am not referring to introverts. Many times introverted people will be mistaken for Wall Flowers. An introvert simply thinks more inwardly as opposed to extroverts, who tend to think out loud with words and actions. In contrast, Wall Flowers are not committed and thus under- perform. To manage them:

- – Find the root cause. Recall our earlier discussion of ability versus motivation. Figure out which best explains the situation and get to work.

- – Make them productive. Identify a big slice of the 80% and put them to work. Sick them on the mundane tasks and hold them accountable.

- – Leave the person alone. This is a very common response and if high performance is your goal you can never choose this option.

- – Fire or remove the person. If the behavior is bad enough and persistent enough, take action as discussed earlier.

- **Prima Donna**. This person is important to the group and has superior skills compared to everyone else. As a result of their ability, they tend to look down on others and become easily irritated and uppity. Long-term, their prima donna attitude will breed conflict and jerk-like behavior. They need to be properly confronted. Consider these steps:

  - – Validate the good. Specify the value added they bring to the table. If you do not start positive, they will not hear you.

  - – Explain the hard-side skill imperfections. Though superior on some skills, they typically are not superior on all skills. No one is perfect and they need to acknowledge this.

– Explain the interpersonal issues. Do not assume they know how they are viewed – positively and specifically explain it to them.

– Clarify expectations. Spell out what you expect future interactions to look like – be very concrete.

CHALLENGE:

Write down the names of the people in your group. Next to each name, write the task or social roles this person typically fills. Identify the biggest holes you see.

If you do not have any short-term control over the group's composition, you will have to coach and cajole others into filling these roles, and step up yourself as well.

The world does not stop if all the good roles are not covered, but in the long-run, on average, you need most of them covered a majority of the time.

Now identify those people in the group who regularly fill the negative roles. For your success and the success of your group, get serious about a plan to better manage these people!

ADDITIONAL CHARACTERISTICS OF HIGH PERFORMING TEAMS

So far we have addressed several crucial factors including team size, staffing, leveraging individuals first, the power of norms, and different key roles.

Beyond this important group of ideas, high performing teams typically possess additional traits as well, including:

- **Shared challenging goals**. Is there a clear and compelling shared goal being pursued? It must be crystal clear in detailed language, understood consistently across members, and be meaningful enough to supersede individual goals

- **Effectively bridge-building skills**. The ability to reach out to individuals and groups not directly involved in your work is a terribly important skill and proof that high performing teams are not simply experts on the task side, but on the soft-skill side as well.

- **Rapid, honest, and constructive communication**. Great teams do not run from conflict, yet they actually do not have much conflict. This is because they are genuinely open to debate and vigorous questioning and discussion. Ideas are not "shot down," they are positively debated.

- **An empowered mindset**. The greatest team ever assembled will fail if they are not given the authority to act. This is a classic leadership maxim: always provide authority commensurate with responsibility. The better the team is and/or the more important their task, the more this is true.

- **Mutual accountability**. This refers to accountability for formal measures and deliverables and for informal norms. Most leaders must rely on the performance management process to maximize productivity. High performing teams have far less need for traditional employee evaluations and similar devices in the face of naturally occurring accountability.

- **Willingness to take calculated risks**. Great teams do not become great by pursuing safe, incremental paths. However, abnormally high performance is not the result of reckless risk-taking. Great teams do their homework, collect the data, confer with the relevant experts, work to control risks, and then set challenging goals in the name of innovation and improvement.

- **High intrinsic motivation**. The best groups are defined by having a strong preponderance of members who are very intrinsically motivated. They love their work and love working together. Under those conditions, many common approaches to extrinsic motivation (e.g., financial incentives) become less important for morale and productivity.

- **Above average skill and experience**. High-performing teams have been successful at attracting, building, and retaining above-average talent. This reduces the need for traditional leadership.

SIGNS YOU ARE SLIPPING INTO MEDIOCRITY

It is important to understand what high- performing teams are and what they look like. However, to be practical, it might be more useful to talk about how to identify a group that is slipping into mediocrity. Take a look at these items and think about your group.

Your team is slipping into mediocrity if:

- **It values civility over candor**. Polite interpersonal relationships are important. However, they can never be more important than actually talking about key performance-related issues.

- **Members like to blame more than admit fault**. You will recall the dreaded BLAME game. If members of the group do not own their share of responsibility for the team's performance, the group will chronically underachieve. No BLAME game.

- **The team allows too much bullying**. If it has become acceptable to belittle people, criticize without helping, or in general to be unproductively negative, mediocrity is just around the corner.

- **Members seek to self-aggrandize instead of helping others**. When individuals spend more time talking about (and working to support) themselves instead of the team, team performance is certain to suffer.

- **Individuals play favorites instead of loving performance**. When friendships begin to explain decision making better than merit, morale and then performance will take a hit.

- **People have more private conversations than public conversations**. When most of the honest and important conversations happen within subgroups, you have succumbed to excessive politics and sacrificed effective group communication.

Of course, the question is what can be done about these issues? Earlier, we addressed many solid answers involving how to motivate others, the performance management process, the need for you to be a great model, and the possible need to instigate positive conflict – any of which might be a part of the solution.

In addition, high-performing teams use these three operational tactics: developing a lieutenant for you as a leader, changing things up to keep things fresh, and running smart meetings.

THE LEADER AND THE LIEUTENANT

Every leader needs a great second-in-command, a lieutenant, a go-to person, call them what you like. It is important that this be an informal understanding, not a formal position. This person is a hedge against your inability to be in two places at once. They provide vital current operational support and fill several other roles as well, including:

- **Standing in for you when needed**. Time is limited and you cannot court every customer or attend every meeting. The lieutenant can help by keeping you in the loop.

- **Initiating followership in tough situations**. Sometimes when tough decisions have been made it is difficult to mobilize support. Once one person shows support, others are more likely to follow. The lieutenant will become a catalyst for support when needed.

- **Serving as a conduit for feedback**. Leaders face information filters that can deeply skew the messages they receive. A solid lieutenant has one foot in the followers' camp and will serve as a source of unfiltered feedback.

- **Being your personal devil's advocate**. We talked about the devil's advocate in a team setting, but here we are referring to someone willing and able to privately question your assumptions when needed. Grant your lieutenant this right.

It is also important to note what a good lieutenant is not:

- **A clone**. They do not have to be the leader's opposite. Some overlap in skills, experience, personality, and background is okay, but with too much similarity, the lieutenant is likely to lose the objectivity required to be a good lieutenant and may be viewed as a carbon copy of the leader.

- **A "yes man."** Yes men tell the leader what they believe the leader wishes to hear. They do not care about great feedback nearly as much as making the leader feel good by offering inaccurate or inappropriate comments or feedback.

- **A future leader**. A good lieutenant may or may not occupy a formal leadership position now or in the future. Some may want to follow your path. Others are more content to be world-class lieutenants instead of shouldering the extra challenges associated with formal leadership roles. Both kinds are acceptable.

CHALLENGE:
Can you identify your lieutenant?

KEEPING THINGS FRESH

Being a leader and facilitating the work of a team is challenging. Even if you understand everything up to this point, performance sometimes stalls out for many reasons:

- **People lose focus on the mission**. Over time, team members cannot see the forest through the trees. As we lose focus on long-term goals, short-term efforts become misaligned.

- **We fall into behavioral ruts**. To cope with the many things to do every day we develop many behavioral routines. Though they create efficiencies, they often lead to a lack of critical thought over time.

- **People's interests change**. The longer the team's tenure, the more people might develop new interests and/or lose interest in tasks which were once intrinsically motivating.

- **The team gets tired!** If you do half of the things suggested in this book, your team is working very hard and pushing themselves to the limit! An occasional bout of mild burnout is not surprising.

- **External conditions change**. The team might be very well structured and functioning at a high level, but then corporate strategy, market conditions, or other unexpected changes take place and the team may no longer be optimized.

As a result, it is important to know how to reenergize a group and keep things fresh. At least four activities are commonly effective:

- **Membership changes**. Small changes to team composition following significant periods of static tenure can support a rejuvenated team atmosphere. New members bring new perspectives and skills and often influence established members to reconsider certain facets of the team's performance and dynamics.

- **Change routines, add new stimuli**. As noted above, time often brings behavioral ruts, but you can shake free of the ruts through role sharing, changing meeting times, eating lunch at new locations – any deviation from deeply established routines is helpful.

- **Provide both group and individual feedback**. Sometimes leaders fall into a pattern of offering only group level feedback. While helpful, this does not provide individuals with specific feedback to support their continued development. Balance the individual and group feedback.

- **Teambuilding retreats**. These activities can be terribly useful if they: are rare instead of common (once per year maximum), are not used simply as a reward, incorporate fun with learning, use a highly-skilled facilitator, start with clear goals in mind, focus on only a small number of issues, and include more than just the "usual suspects."

RUN SMART MEETINGS

Most meetings are unnecessary and are not run correctly. Follow the rules below to reduce the total number of hours you and your team spend in meetings while simultaneously increasing meeting productivity.

**Meetings are not evil.
Unnecessary meetings and
poorly run meetings are evil.**

When to Call a Meeting

The first rule of meetings: when in doubt, do not call a meeting. Sadly, in practice, the opposite is often true.

Note: meeting on a regularly scheduled basis for the sake of it is not a defensible rationale.

Below are the major justifications for calling a meeting. If your rationale is not on the list below, seriously consider using electronic collaboration tools to make progress, or have subgroups meet to discuss the issue.

- **Make key decisions**. Meet for big decisions (in the 20%) when the team expects to have a strong say in the matter.

- **Seek input for key decisions**. When the leader will make the call, yet needs genuine input and support for a key decision, a meeting may be justified.

- **Kick-off**. For larger initiatives, a kick-off meeting is useful to socialize, ensure clarity of purpose, set norms, clarify roles, and clarify goals.

- **Premortem**. A meeting that is recommended for larger efforts that is dedicated to predicting and imagining what might fail or go wrong with your plan. This is the time to plan for how to address the worst possibilities.

- **Postmortem**. Following major task or project completion, this meeting is dedicated to understanding what went well and what did not. What is learned must somehow be captured and institutionalized in order to benefit future efforts.

Also, given the busy nature of most professionals' schedules, it is not always feasible for all team members to be present when a meeting is called. At the group's inception, agree upon the size of a reasonable quorum.

You always need genuine input from your team, but try not to let one person's absence stop you from scheduling a needed meeting.

Who to Invite

Focus on small meetings. Strive to minimize the levels of hierarchy present in any given meeting. Generally, the fewer levels present, the more robust the conversation.

CHALLENGE:

The golden rule of invitations: when in doubt, do not invite the person.

There are three main types of people to invite to a meeting: the experts, the affected, and the sponsors.

- **The experts**. They are the people with knowledge and talent relative to the topic at hand. Keep in mind the need for as few participants as possible.

- **The affected**. Consider the issues to be addressed at the meeting: which outside people or groups will you need to have data or help from and how will your work affect the work of others later? A small number of those whom might be affected can make great meeting participants.

- **The sponsors**. All meetings need a sponsor (a higher-level person who openly supports the project). The more important the effort, the more you must clarify sponsorship and occasionally have them attend to keep them in the loop and to solidify sponsorship.

The Actual Meeting

Let's start with the balance of social interaction versus work-related interaction at a meeting. Many leaders love efficiency and thus err on too little social banter. Most employees prefer modest amounts of social banter. Consider the following:

- **Begin the meeting with social chit chat**. Two or three minutes of quality social interaction is the grease that smoothes the way for productively discussing the actual tasks at hand for the majority of the meeting.

- **If things turn social, do not panic**. During the meeting, for whatever reason, if the conversation turns away from work and towards outside social issues, do not immediately squash the diversion. Again, two or three minutes here can ensure many subsequent minutes on task.

- **End on a social note**. After all business is wrapped up, consider ending with a reminder about the upcoming company event, a heartfelt comment about enjoying the weekend, or a warm congratulations to someone about to have a baby or close on a house – something personal and social.

Strive for effective flow. Resist beginning your meetings with boring repetitive reporting of "updates" from all members. Most updates should be electronically distributed and digested prior to the meeting. At the meeting you look for help and/or affirmation concerning:

- Decisions made
- Options being considered
- Roadblocks encountered
- Late breaking information

In general, when you speak up, you provide the group what it needs to know, erring on fewer details.

Your focus is not to have them understand every last aspect of your recent work, but to have them understand your contribution to the group's work.

The rules. When the focus shifts to the task at hand, remember: all effective meetings follow certain rules. Meeting rules are similar to norms discussed earlier, yet they are more focused and directed specifically at meetings as opposed to group behavior in general.

Agree upon the rules when the meeting begins (after any initial social interactions) and be willing and able to speak up when the group is in jeopardy of violating one of the rules.

There is no perfect set of rules, though common rules might address:

- **Nailing the boundaries**. Start by stating the goal for the meeting and any general comments about the scope of the topics to be addressed.

- **When to start**. Not only when to start, but the need to be on time.

- **When to stop**. You can either stop at the designated time or when the work is complete. The best answer depends on deadlines and the quality of the meeting.

- **Behaviors**. This includes both acceptable and unacceptable behaviors during the meeting. Be very specific. For example, no phone calls, no texts, etc.

- **Decision rules**. These may be the same as the decision rules the group always uses, or new, tailored to address the specific nature of the meeting.

- **Homework**. All members commit to arriving having completed any assigned reading or other work and with all materials in hand.

- **Penalties**. This can be fun, but is vital – not adhering to rules must have consequences. It might be as simple as having to put a dollar in the team's lunch fund. Consider different penalties for different rules.

The tools. In addition to playful and helpful penalties, you can make your rules more effective by using a variety of tools. The two most important tools are the agenda and the parking lot.

Contrary to popular opinion, creating and using an

agenda does not have to be complex. However, it must be clear and facilitated correctly. Note these core elements and issues concerning meeting agendas:

- **The responsible person.** Allow no ambiguity. Someone must own the process of assembling the agenda.

- **A schedule.** Anyone who wishes to contribute to the agenda must know the due date and, with rare exceptions, it needs to be a hard date.

- **The order of agenda items.** Never allow an agenda to be used politically by hiding items late in the list. Always address the important issues immediately.

- **Agenda integrity.** It is important to adhere to the list of issues on the agenda. There might be occasional exceptions, but this is a great rule. When an issue is relevant, but not relevant right now, consider putting it in the parking lot.

The agenda is complemented by the parking lot. It is common for work-related tangents to pop up during meetings. Not all tangents are created equal. You will have to decide, but, like social banter, try not to start by squashing tangents as irrelevant.

When you listen for a moment and decide the tangent is too far off base, it is time to use the parking lot. The parking lot is a place you "park" an idea or issue that has merit and likely needs attention, but is too far out of scope for the current meeting.

The parking lot cannot simply be a group of ideas and issues in someone's mind. It needs to be physical. It could be many things such as a:

- White board
- Group of post-it notes
- Pad of paper
- Flip chart
- Computer file

The parking lot might seem like a simple device, but it is very important. Effective use of the parking lot will:

- **Keep you on track**. Proper use of the lot will allow maximum time to continue making progress that is directly relevant to the agenda.

- **Validate others' points**. If someone's comment is taking the meeting out of scope, the parking lot is a positive way to affirm the importance of what they are saying and the importance of their contribution, thus keeping them engaged in the meeting.

- **Provide a repository**. The parking lot becomes the known place to go when ideas need to be revisited. It is an established reference point for future work and future meetings.

Like any tool, the parking lot can be abused. To ensure that everyone views the parking lot as legitimate and helpful, be sure not to:

- **Use it too quickly**. Do not pass judgment without hearing the person's entire idea. Do not be hasty.

- **Use it politically**. Do not allow anyone to park ideas in the lot simply to avoid making decisions they do not support.

- **Forget it exists**. If you use the lot properly but fail to ever revisit it and pick up needed ideas at the right time, people will see it as a graveyard instead of a parking lot and its utility will cease.

Aside from the agenda and the parking lot, do not be afraid to explore more simple but useful tools to reinforce your norms and keep you on track. Imagine the possibilities with Nerf balls, whoopee cushions, squirt guns, squeaky dog toys, and egg timers – you name it.

The roles. Beyond normal team roles there are two additional roles to consider for effective meetings:

- **The facilitator**. This person is a process observer who attends to the norms, the rules, and the agenda. They encourage others when needed to ensure the group achieves positive and productive progress. This person does not have to be the highest status person – merely a willing and able facilitator who monitors and manages the meeting process.

- **The scribe**. The scribe is the meeting archivist. This person captures the main topics addressed, major comments from the members, the conclusions drawn, tasks assigned, etc. Later, when wrapping the meeting, and even later following the meeting, the information collected by the scribe serves as an objective check against fuzzy memories. A good scribe helps keep people honest and on track.

Tricks and tips. There are many operational tactics that help support meeting effectiveness. There are many variations of methods such as these:

- **Perpetual homework**. One of the best ways to create momentum in a meeting is for some of the work to be done before anyone arrives. Idea generation, data analysis, or some other form of pre-work is almost always possible and helps give the group a running start.

- **Rotate roles**. There are several common roles including the devil's advocate, the scribe, the person who runs the agenda, etc. Mix them up and ask someone to fill a role that they commonly do not fill.

- **Keep score**. Have a person, other than the scribe, keep score to see how often certain norms are violated, and by whom. Post it on a wall – visual management is a great aid for behavior change!

- **Change times and place**. One reason ruts happen is due to over familiarity with physical surroundings. Meet in a different room, outside, or at a coffee shop a couple times each year – mix it up.

How to End a Meeting

Do not end a meeting by finding a breaking point, declaring that it has been an hour, and dismissing the participants. If you want to maximize the value added by your meetings, be sure to end by:

- **Stating agreements**. Articulate what has been accomplished and agreed to by the team. Make sure there is no ambiguity.

- **Stating what is not yet complete**. Clarify exactly what is not yet complete and gain agreement.

- **Stating new/ongoing responsibilities**. Concretely state who is to continue and/or start which tasks and when they are due.

- **Discussing the next meeting**. Either agree that it needs to be scheduled now or agree who will coordinate the scheduling of the next meeting when it becomes necessary. In the latter case, explicitly state when it will be necessary to have another meeting – clearly identify the conditions.

- **Taking questions**. Always provide time to ask questions for clarification – people expect it.

- **Offering a social comment**. As noted earlier, a great way to end is to spend a few seconds offering a genuine non-task comment (e.g., about the weekend). Our work lives exist within our larger lives and referencing that reality often helps others keep perspective.

CLOSING THOUGHTS

This book is not the last word on leadership. It is the first word. Every simple idea, paragraph, or bullet list can be explored in far more detail via many additional resources. This book is only your guide to seeing how all of the major parts of leadership fit together.

As you continue your leadership journey, I would like to reiterate a few crucial ideas and share a couple new ones. As you continue to develop, keep the following in mind:

- **Leadership is about skills not birthright**. While some traits help, the truth is most of your leadership success will be explained by hard work and your mastery of the skills described in this book.

- **The cumulative effect**. Stop looking for home runs and remember that leadership success is best defined as the cumulative effect of many small things done correctly over time.

- **Marathon not a sprint**. Do not attempt to master all of this over night. Get it right a piece at a time and assume a good pace, but one that you can maintain. You want to finish the marathon.

- **Keep the conversation alive**. You personally have the power to not only continue your professional development, but that of others as well. Use the book as a conversation starter for a book club, brown bag lunch series, or an online discussion group. Keep these topics alive and actively considered by your leadership team.

To secure Dr. Dewett for speaking or other engagements, or to order discounted bulk quantities of this book, email Todd at todd@drdewett.com, or call 800 401 2926. Please visit us at www.drdewett.com!